inclusion

THE NEW
COMPETITIVE
BUSINESS
ADVANTAGE

SHIRLEY ENGELMEIER

InclusionINC Media
Minneapolis, MN

Published by
InclusionINC Media
126 North 3rd Street, Suite 412
Minneapolis, MN 55401
www.inclusionincmedia.com

Publisher's Cataloging-in-Publication Data
Engelmeier, Shirley.

Inclusion : the new competitive business advantage / Shirley Engelmeier. – Minneapolis, MN : InclusionINC Media, 2012.

p. ; cm.

ISBN13: 978-0-9860037-0-7

1. Diversity in the workplace. 2. Personnel management. 3. Manpower planning. I. Title.

HF5549.5.M5 E54 2012
658.3008—dc23   2012935081

FIRST EDITION

Project coordination by Jenkins Group, Inc.
www.BookPublishing.com

Interior design by Brooke Camfield

Printed in the United States of America
16   15   14   13   12   •   5   4   3   2   1

Dedication

To my mom and dad, Mary and Larry Engelmeier, two farm kids from rural Minnesota who taught me that hard work and doing the right thing always pay off and that good things happen to good people; it's just a question of *when*. I love you beyond words.

Contents

INCLUSION

Foreword

Why Inclusion Matters

For nearly twenty years, I've worked with organizations to address workforce changes as an inclusion and diversity consultant. Prior to that, I spent more than fifteen years in large organizations including Brown & Williamson and Frito-Lay. Ultimately, I opted out of Corporate America and eventually began my own consulting firm to avoid the hardships required of women in pursuit of career advancement at that time. Yet here we are, twenty years later, with little progress to show for the broad-based effort that has been called diversity.

In the last few years, as the recession has taken hold, I've seen diversity initiatives thrown under the bus in cost-cutting measures because the business linkage had not been made. This is highly unfortunate, because that linkage is more valuable now than ever!

For years, much of Corporate America has been stuck on the concept of diversity—i.e., race and gender—and hasn't gotten the bigger picture of changing the workplace culture to one of inclusion that leverages the benefits of diversity for business gains. More significantly, inclusion and diversity haven't been treated as mission critical; they haven't been linked to business outcomes.

Two tactics that have been employed under the diversity umbrella are a targeted focus on recruitment strategies and a singular emphasis on training. While hiring women and people of color is a historic tactic for achieving a diverse workforce, it is not a primary strategy for driving change. Targeted hiring remains critical, but no sustainable change will occur until senior leaders leverage the business connection between diversity and the bottom line. Hiring women and people of color has never been important simply for the sake of political correctness or because it is "the right thing to do." The goal has always been a double edged sword—attracting and retaining the best talent for the benefit of the business as well as opening the doors of opportunity across the entire demographic spectrum.

The other tactic that has been broadly but ineffectively used is training. The one-time training event that occurs every three to seven years (a "dip and done" approach) has seen better days. Corporate America has needed and still needs an accelerated learning strategy associated with new business behaviors and a new underlying paradigm of what inclusion and yes, diversity, mean to business success.

I began working in this arena twenty years ago, cutting my teeth on Denny's Consent Decree. My esteemed colleagues and I worked for two and a half years to correct the ills of a major class action lawsuit. In the mid '90s we were already talking about inclusion and diversity as keys to business success. When I founded InclusionINC more than a decade ago, the brand promise was highly focused on the critical importance of inclusion as key to business success because it was clear even then that diversity by itself was only part of the story.

While diversity is certainly linked to inclusion, organizations can be diverse and not inclusive. This body of work began with a primary focus on race, gender, and representation metrics; that's the diversity side of it. Inclusion is the other side of the diversity coin, and yet inclusion is so much bigger than that.

Today, the reality is that diversity goes beyond race and gender to include the coexistence of four generational cohorts of workers at a time when everyone's voice is needed to drive employee engagement, productivity, and market agility. Today, diversity encourages a global mindset and addresses cross cultural issues. Today, diversity creates inclusive communications that drive innovation.

Inclusion, in turn, is about forming a business strategy and culture that:

- Harnesses great ideas to drive innovation
- Expands business thinking to a global mindset for workforce, workplace, and customers
- Considers every single person in the organization as a knowledge worker
- Says, "Shouldn't inclusion be for everyone?"®
- Embraces the technology and collaborative savvy brought to our organizations by members of Gen Y (also known as Millennials), those born between 1980–2000

Chapters 1–5 in *Inclusion: The New Competitive Business Advantage* highlight the many critical issues facing organizations today, while Chapter 6 talks about the shift to inclusion. Finally, Chapters 7–12 explore how inclusion is a business imperative for these critical issues.

I hope this book helps you embrace the significant difference inclusion can make in the success of your business in the twenty-first century. Your success depends on it.

Acknowledgments

A large and talented cast assisted with this book, including a number of brilliant businesspeople who contributed their wisdom regarding the necessity of inclusion as a competitive business advantage. To do justice to their accomplishments would have added twenty pages to the book. Instead, I have used their words to breathe life into the concept of inclusion. Cindy Bigner, Clydie Douglass, Kelly Elkin, Donald Fan, Kim Koonce, Clarence Nunn, Michael Reid, Rebecca Robinson, and Shanequa Williams and Keith Wyche. I thank each of you with a debt of gratitude too large to put into words.

Closer to home, a heartfelt thank you to my dedicated team for carrying me over the finish line on this project any number of times. Thanks specifically to Bill, Debbie, Jacqui, Kevin, Maria,

Phyllis, and Taylor. You walk the talk with me every day in this important work. Thank you for keeping the faith and for knowing that what we do truly makes a difference.

To Lin Grensing-Pophal and Mike Greece, my co-editors, thank you for your critical thinking skills, endless patience, and on-going optimism. To Justin Grenseng, thank you for your research and organizational skills. Also, a special thanks to Taylor Adams for the terrific design of this book cover.

And finally, thank you to the men in my life. To my husband Russ, thank you for being a gentle spirit who balances me. To my older son John Michael, the most stunning young person I know, and my younger son Zach, a brilliant STEM mind just beginning to make his mark, thank you for illuminating my world.

Introduction

Why This Book?
Why Now?

Asilent but steady transformation is under way in the demographics of the U.S. and ultimately the American workforce. The steady increase in diverse workers replacing a historically white population—a shift unlikely just twenty years ago—now marks a new and potentially defining moment in the nation's cultural, geographic, and business DNA: by the middle of this century, the U.S. Census Bureau estimates that minorities will make up nearly fifty percent of the population.

More importantly, the resulting change in population is inexorably linked to the current and future competiveness of American enterprise. Now more than ever, inclusion must form an integral part of corporate business strategy and culture. The workplace that embraces and leverages variations in perceptions, ideas, and knowledge experiences a level of engagement that can energize productivity, retain highly talented workers, and significantly improve business outcomes.

Though increasing differences in workforce populations make inclusion a significantly more urgent concept than ever before, its highly measureable value is for the most part severely underappreciated. Inclusion remains separate from the strategic part of doing business today. Yet when integrated into the DNA and overall culture of an organization, inclusion can provide a catalyst to gain access to new markets and to attract and keep talent with fresh ideas. But the real benefits are reaped when organizations harness, engage, and connect disparate ideas and experiences to drive productivity, innovation, and competitiveness.

Inclusion begins with the creation of a safe, collaborative workplace ecosystem that supports mutual understanding, expression, and regard for different perspectives. Leaders must demonstrate a corporate and holistic commitment to foster this kind of environment, guide the creation of an inclusive culture, and actively align inclusion initiatives with business strategies.

The concept of inclusion extends beyond creating a workplace that focuses solely on representation metrics. It requires the development of formal and informal mechanisms that invite participation and foster genuine contribution to an enterprise's success.

Inclusion works. Companies with highly integrated and engaged employees demonstrate significantly stronger bottom-line results. This is particularly true when an organization's inclusion initiatives are purposely tied to the objectives and mission of the business.

Given our rapidly changing and increasingly uncertain external and internal business environments, there has never been a greater need to hear what all of your employees think—*not merely your senior leadership team*. There has never been a greater need for all voices and ideas to be heard. There has never been a greater need for inclusion.

Business leaders must find a way to capture the insights and visions of people who reflect the growing diversity of consumers, suppliers, and business partners that span the globe. Managers must consider what they may be doing—or not doing—to attract employees and customers in a global context, even if their business is solely focused on U.S. markets. They must learn to harness the collective ideas of the organization to drive business success and create a business ecosystem worth joining.

We now live and work in an environment where:

- We are faced with great uncertainty from a variety of forces, both economic and natural.
- We are faced with the convergence of technology and new thought processes being brought to the workforce by the younger, highly influential knowledge workers of Gen Y who want to participate, not just execute.
- We are faced with the need to continually innovate and use all of our assets to keep up with domestic and global competition.
- We are faced with radical demographic changes, both in the U.S. and globally, that affect our competitiveness and our markets.

Yet the vast majority of U.S. companies are under-competitive because of a confluence of four conditions:

1. Long-standing business practices that often lock managers into old command and control performance and operational models that aren't inclusive
2. Lack of a strategic linkage between workplace demography and business outcomes
3. Technology that, unlike in any other era, has made it possible for customers, suppliers, and employees to communicate in ways never expected
4. Diverse employees who, despite the gains made by diversity initiatives of the past, remain in lower tiers of business where their influence is much less than that of senior managers

Against the backdrop of these conditions and the tsunami-like changes occurring in the demography of the United States, this book suggests that organizations can realize huge benefits deploying Inclusion as a Business Strategy®, thereby creating a business culture that *includes* the perspectives of people who don't think like us and often don't look like us, talk like us, or have the same perspectives as us.

Inclusion: The New Competitive Business Advantage can aid businesses and their leaders in this critical endeavor.

1

The Radical Seismic Demographic Shift

What I've noticed in diversity strategies is that if you're struggling, it's probably because you're fishing in the wrong ponds. I literally had this conversation last week with a headhunter who said they were having a hard time finding a person of color for a certain position. I said, 'Have you talked to people at the Executive Leadership Council? They're made up of the three hundred highest ranking African Americans. Have you talked to people from Hacer? They work with Latinos. You're struggling, but you haven't developed the relationships; you're not aware.' If you're serious, you have to understand where that talent is and how to connect to it because they're just not going to walk up and knock on your door.

Keith Wyche,
President and CEO,
Cub Foods

The most recent 2010 U.S. Census should send shockwaves to organizations across the country, and yet it hasn't. Why? In part, the reality that our workforce will look vastly different in just fifteen years is troubling. Few companies are actually prepared for the aging and "browning" of America. Reports published by the U.S. Department of Labor, the Urban League, and the Pew Center for Hispanic Research prompt little action from Corporate America to meet the reality of the changing workforce, changing customers, and emerging markets.

In the mid '90s, significant time and effort was spent on Workforce 2000, a groundbreaking report that for the first time shed light on the changes that were going to occur regarding race and ethnicity in America. But the time for projections is over; the change is here!

The past ten years have seen progressive companies begin planning to address an impending "war for talent" that will occur when the Baby Boomers (those born between 1946-1964) retire. Nonetheless, a significant part of Corporate America has received a reprieve thanks to the recession and the slowness of the recovery. Concern about talent wars has moved off the radar screen as most organizations have entered "survival mode" in an attempt to navigate the worst financial situation since the Great Depression. This has created a short-term illusion that retaining talent is no longer an issue.

From 2008 to the present, many employees have been happy just to have a job. Boomers have had to alter their life plans and stay employed longer than expected as they watched retirement savings dwindle in the tough economy.

And yet we know that, inevitably, these demographic changes are going to catch up with Corporate America. We know that as the Baby Boomers reach retirement age in growing numbers, they will be replaced by the employees of Gen Y, also known as the Millennials. A corresponding bubble can be seen in the under eighteen age segment.

Compounding the issue is that the educational requirements for knowledge workers today are much higher than they were for the Baby Boomers. Once again, the confluence of factors of both an increasingly diverse and an increasingly older population should set off alarms across America.

Even more compelling is how rapidly the management style will need to change. When Boomers began their work, they expected to be told what to do and to do it, a reflection of the classic "command and control" management style; but gone are the days when leaders could command mindless support from their followers simply by virtue of their position within an organization. Today's new generation of workers wants to know *why* they are being asked to do something, and not only why it's important to the organization but also why it's important to them and, often, to society at large.

THE AGING OF THE U.S. POPULATION

Let's look first at the aging population. As the following graph shows, the median age of the U.S. population has been growing dramatically since 1990 and isn't expected to level out until 2050. There will soon be five generations in the workplace, fueling the need to fully understand and include perspectives from each of these generations.

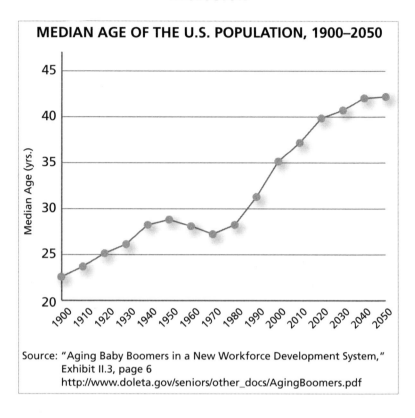

MEDIAN AGE OF THE U.S. POPULATION, 1900–2050

Source: "Aging Baby Boomers in a New Workforce Development System,"
Exhibit II.3, page 6
http://www.doleta.gov/seniors/other_docs/AgingBoomers.pdf

At the same time, the proportion of minorities in the U.S. is increasing significantly. The Selig Center for Economic Growth estimates that there will be close to seventy million non-whites in the U.S. by the year 2015, an increase of seventy-two percent from 1990. A significant portion of that growth has come from the Hispanic population, which grew from 35.3 million Americans in 1980 to 50.5 million in 2010.[1] From 1980-2020, Caucasian workers in the U.S. will decline from eighty-two to sixty-three percent while the non-Caucasian proportion of the workforce will double from eighteen to thirty-seven percent.[2]

These workers were previously called the "minority"; today they represent the majority in many cities and states. The more accurate reference to this growing population is "people of color," and they are well represented among the Gen Y generation, which will disproportionately represent the greatest influence in the workforce. Hispanics alone represented 23.1 percent of the under eighteen age group in the U.S. as of 2010.[3] By contrast, non-Hispanic whites are projected to be the slowest growing group. From 1990-2000, the non-Hispanic white population represented thirty-five percent of the total U.S. population growth. Between 1990-2030, the U.S. Census Bureau expects that number to fall to fourteen percent, with this group actually decreasing in size after 2030.[4]

The following graph shows the dramatic nature of the change. In just the past decade, the "white alone" population had the smallest percentage of increase, at 5.7%. The greatest change is the 43% increase in the Hispanic or Latino population.

NATIONAL POPULATION BY RACE
UNITED STATES: 2010

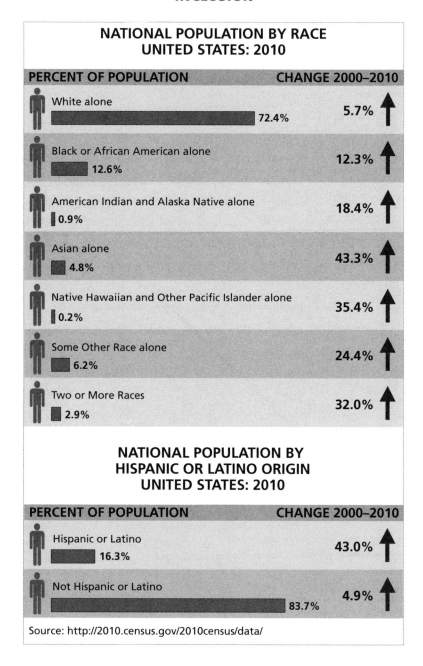

PERCENT OF POPULATION — **CHANGE 2000–2010**

White alone — 72.4% — 5.7% ↑

Black or African American alone — 12.6% — 12.3% ↑

American Indian and Alaska Native alone — 0.9% — 18.4% ↑

Asian alone — 4.8% — 43.3% ↑

Native Hawaiian and Other Pacific Islander alone — 0.2% — 35.4% ↑

Some Other Race alone — 6.2% — 24.4% ↑

Two or More Races — 2.9% — 32.0% ↑

NATIONAL POPULATION BY
HISPANIC OR LATINO ORIGIN
UNITED STATES: 2010

PERCENT OF POPULATION — **CHANGE 2000–2010**

Hispanic or Latino — 16.3% — 43.0% ↑

Not Hispanic or Latino — 83.7% — 4.9% ↑

Source: http://2010.census.gov/2010census/data/

We have reached the tipping point.

The long-term impact of the changes in growth is further evident when looking at the trend analysis that follows. By 2050, the U.S. Census projects that non-Hispanic whites will make up 52.5% of the population. At this point, nearly half of the U.S. population will be racially or ethnically different than it was just a short time ago.

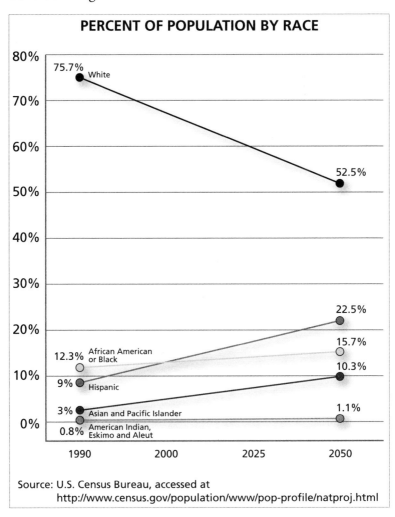

PERCENT OF POPULATION BY RACE

80%

75.7% White

70%

60%

52.5%

50%

40%

30%

22.5%

20%

15.7%

12.3% African American or Black

10.3%

10%

9% Hispanic

3% Asian and Pacific Islander

1.1%

0%

0.8% American Indian, Eskimo and Aleut

1990   2000   2025   2050

Source: U.S. Census Bureau, accessed at
http://www.census.gov/population/www/pop-profile/natproj.html

Clearly, businesses today are dealing with a constantly changing mix of people and perspectives that often present challenges, both for management and for employees themselves. Shifts are happening in gender, age, and ethnicity; these factors impact the make-up of the workplace and the population at large.

These seismic demographic shifts in the U.S. population hold both peril and promise for Corporate America. They hold peril for those who fail to recognize and take steps to embrace the diversity of a changing employee and customer landscape, but they hold promise for those who, through inclusion, can capitalize on the significant potential these populations hold for them.

BUYING POWER/U.S. EMERGING MARKETS

Not only will these demographic shifts have important implications for the make-up of the future workforce but they will also influence the corporate customer base. The Selig Center for Economic Growth indicates that the impact of diverse markets will be significant. Let's take a closer look at the numbers below.

Diverse Markets—U.S. Buyer Power[5]

- Women = $5 trillion
- Hispanic/Latino = $1.036 trillion
- African American = $957 billion
- Gay/Lesbian = $759 billion
- Asian American = $544 billion
- Multiracial = $116 billion
- Native American = $68 billion
- Disabled = $461 billion
- Mature = $1.1 trillion

In 2015, African-Americans will account for 8.8 percent of all U.S. buying power, up from 7.4 percent in 1990. In 2015, Hispanics will account for 9.9 percent of all U.S. buying power, up from five percent in 1990. In 2015, Asians will account for 5.5 percent of all U.S. buying power, up from 2.7 percent in 1990.[6] What's more, those numbers are likely to grow exponentially over the next decade.

This paints a picture of the potential for a rapidly changing consumer demand for products and services that meets the expectations of a wide range of market segments that have never before been served in the U.S. At the same time, businesses in the U.S. are no longer just impacted by the U.S. economy. They are increasingly impacted by an equally rapidly growing and interactive global economy as well.

What do I see happening on a global level? Emerging markets and rapidly changing global consumerism are creating an economic imperative that seems evident to most businesses. Yet, while apparent, this opportunity is not so readily addressed. The disconnect occurs because the employee population needs to be reflective of the new and emerging consumer both in the U.S. and globally. Inclusion is necessary to tap these opportunities, but the dots, to date, have not been connected.

Endnotes

1. "Census 2010: 50 Million Latinos." D'Vera Cohn, Jeffrey Passel, and Mark Hugo Lopez. Pew Hispanic Center, March 24, 2011.

2. "A National Dialogue: The Secretary of Education's Commission on the Future of Higher Education." See http://www2.ed.gov/about/bdscomm/list/hiedfuture/reports/equity.pdf.

3. "Hispanics Account for More Than Half of Nation's Growth in Past Decade." D'Vera Coh, Jeffrey Passel and Mark Hugo Lopez. Pew Hispanic Center, March 24, 2011.

4. "Population Profile of the United States." Jennifer Cheeseman Day. U.S. Census Bureau.

5. Selig Center for Economic Growth, University of Georgia, 2010.

6. Ibid.

2
The Global Mindset

The global economy and emerging markets create unique opportunities and challenges for global companies.

Clydie Douglass,
Director Diversity and Inclusion,
3M

We look at how we can truly enhance these competencies around a global culture—how we can be sensitive and able to lead with the nuances from the culture perspective as well as be open-minded and nimble.

Donald Fan,
Senior Director, Global Office of Diversity,
Walmart

INCLUSION

Just as the buying power of the newly emerging and increasingly diverse populations in America is projected to change significantly over the next few decades, the ability of citizens of less developed nations to purchase consumer goods and services is also projected to markedly increase between now and 2050.

John Hawksworth of PricewaterhouseCoopers shows compelling evidence of this shift in *The World in 2050*. The following chart shows the dramatic change from 2005-2050 for some of the world's largest developing economies. The current G7 (U.S., Japan, Germany, UK, France, Italy and Canada), plus Spain, Australia and South Korea is compared with the emerging E7 (China, India, Brazil, Russia, Indonesia, Mexico and Turkey).

The 17 largest economies in the world are compared in purchasing power parity (PPP) and market exchange rates (MER). You don't have to be an economist to see the huge shift! As Hawksworth notes: "The E7 economies will by 2050 be around 25 percent larger than the current G7 when measured in dollar terms at MER, or around 75 percent larger in PPP terms. In contrast, the E7 is currently only around 20 percent of the size of the G7 at market exchange rates and around 75 percent of its size in PPP terms."[1]

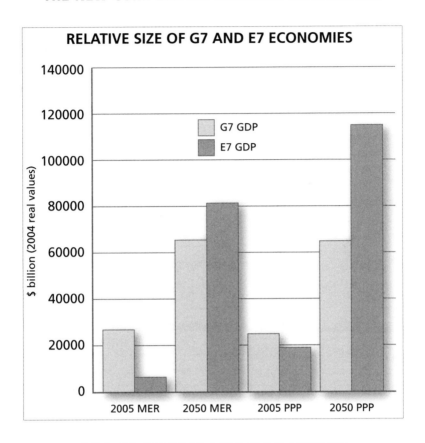

RELATIVE SIZE OF G7 AND E7 ECONOMIES

CHANGES IN ECONOMIC INFLUENCE

Any doubt that the global market is having an impact on the success of companies here in the U.S. disappears by looking at data showing where the top company headquarters are located. The number of companies headquartered in the U.S. declined by twenty-four percent between 2005-2011, while the number of companies headquartered in China has increased by 281 percent! Jeanne Meister and Karie Willyerd in *The 2020 Workplace* predict that by 2020, the BRIC countries (Brazil, Russia, India, and China) will be the dominant centers of economic influence.

The following chart shows the fastest growing by percentage on the top. Sadly, the United States trails the pack while China has a clear lead!

CHANGES IN GLOBAL 500 COMPANY HEADQUARTERS—WHO'S WINNING?

Country	2005	2006	2007	2008	2009	2010	2011	% Change	Net Inc/Decr 2005–2011
China	16	20	24	29	37	46	61	281	45
Brazil	3	4	5	5	6	7	7	133	4
Russia	3	5	4	5	8	6	7	133	4
India	5	6	6	7	7	8	8	60	3
Switzerland	11	12	13	14	15	15	15	36	4
Italy	8	10	10	10	10	11	10	25	2
Spain	8	9	9	11	12	10	9	13	1
Germany	37	35	37	37	39	37	34	-8	-3
France	39	38	38	39	40	39	35	-10	-4
Australia	9	8	8	8	9	8	8	-11	-1
Britain	35	38	33	34	26	29	30	-14	-5
Netherlands	14	14	14	13	12	13	12	-14	-2
Canada	13	14	16	14	14	11	11	-15	-2
Japan	81	70	67	64	68	71	68	-16	-13
United States	176	170	162	153	140	139	133	-24	-43

Source: *Financial Times* Global 500—Top Fifteen Countries

There is no question that global trade is of critical importance to the United States and other countries as they seek to be competitive in a world economy. What is hampering the United States' efforts to capitalize on these world markets? I suggest it is the failure to first capitalize on the power of employees.

This must be a mindful process. As Cindy Bigner, Director, Global Diversity and Inclusion at Halliburton, notes, "We, as a company, put forth a lot of effort to make sure we are nationalized as much as possible. That means that we hire local nationals from countries wherever possible. That creates a whole different view, if you will."

That said, she acknowledges that, "Our biggest issue and the problem that other companies also have is that we're not getting nationalized employees in the higher ranks. Our focus has been on getting them trained for high-level positions."

Our current U.S. workforce does not reflect the face of this changing market. As emerging markets grow, we need to consider whether our existing workforce can address emerging global needs. In many cases today, it cannot.

The Forbes Insights report, "Global Diversity and Inclusion: Fostering Innovation Through a Diverse Workforce," indicated that:

- Diversity is a key driver of innovation and a critical component of being successful on a global scale.
- A diverse and inclusive workforce is crucial for companies that want to attract and retain top talent.

Yet, despite these findings, the report also indicated that organizations' diversity goals and priorities won't change significantly over the next three years and that, while significant progress has been made to build and retain diverse workforces, there are still significant inroads to be made.

The report concludes, "The globalization of business has created a sophisticated, complex and competitive environment. In order to be successful, companies need to continually create new products and services. And the best way to ensure the development of new ideas is through a diverse and inclusive workforce."[2]

Relying on your current workforce to reach new markets may work in the short term, but as markets evolve, businesses will need to call upon an increasingly technologically savvy and connected global workforce. This is not and cannot be a U.S.-centric model.

To capture emerging markets, businesses need to develop a highly engaged global workforce and mindset that understands:

- Who their current customers are
- Who their emerging customers are
- What their current and emerging customers' needs, values, and preferences are
- Why and how their customers access their services
- How to communicate effectively with their customers
- How to customize products and services based on demand

Donald Fan, Senior Director, Global Office of Diversity at Walmart, says, "In the old retail models, whatever you buy you can sell. It means you can push whatever you want to the customer. But today, it is a customer-driven market and the customer makes the decisions about what they want. In order to gain that kind of customer insight, you've got to have a truly diverse workforce."

As Robert Safian, editor of *Fast Company*, wrote in his January 2012 article "This Is Generation Flux," he points out "the pace of disruption is roaring ahead." While there is much uncertainty, he notes: "There is one certainty, however. The next decade or two will be defined more by fluidity than by any new, settled paradigm; if there is a pattern to all this, it is that there is no pattern."

Businesses wishing to survive in this climate, he predicts, will need to take an entirely different approach. Some will survive. These he calls "Generation Flux" and says: "What defines

GenFlux is a mindset that embraces instability, that tolerates—and even enjoys—recalibrating careers, business models and assumptions. Not everyone will join Generation Flux, but to be successful, businesses and individuals will have to work at it."[3]

This is the new business normal. Until organizations can respond effectively to the new normal, *nobody* wins:

- Not the employees who are unable to lend their expertise and passion in support of their organizations' marketing

- Not the organizations that hire diverse workers but don't involve them

- Not the customers whose experiences with various organizations might have been more valuable if those organizations had listened to the voices of *all* their constituents

Let's say you're a U.S.-based multinational company that is expanding to Brazil. Do you put a manager in place for your Brazilian operations from your U.S. operation, or do you staff that position with a local national? Who is more likely to understand the market? And how do you make product and service decisions?

According to a PricewaterhouseCoopers survey of over 1,400 CEOs of major international companies, twenty-eight percent said they had developed or planned to develop unique products for the Russian market, thirty-two percent said the same for the Brazilian and Indian markets, and forty percent said they had developed or planned to develop unique products for the Chinese market.[4] Below are some examples of products developed for specific international markets:

- Coca-Cola with Lime is available in Belgium, the Netherlands, Singapore, Canada, the United Kingdom, and the U.S.
- Coca-Cola with Raspberry was only available in New Zealand until 2009, when it was also made available in the U.S. through the Coca-Cola Freestyle touch-screen fountain
- Coca-Cola Light Sango (a blood-orange flavor) is only available in France and Belgium
- Coca-Cola Citra is available in Mexico and Japan
- McDonald's McArabia—grilled chicken or kofta wrapped in pita—is available throughout the Middle East
- McDonald's Ebi Filet-O Shrimp burger is available in Japan
- McDonald's Dulce de Leche ice cream is available in South America
- Green Tea Oreos are available in China
- Avon, Procter & Gamble, and L'Oreal all have ethnic products

Consumer product companies like Coca-Cola, Procter & Gamble, and Avon are not only learning how they might change their existing products and services to accommodate all customers but also that those new insights can increase market share to existing untapped new markets.

Consider some of the changes in the food products available at U.S. grocery stores that have been impacted by the growing Hispanic population. These global impacts range from restaurants like Abuelos, Chevys, El Pollo Loco, and Chili's to food products now flavored with chipotle, cilantro, chilies, cumin, and lime. The fact that masa, a prime ingredient for making tamales, is available at some Walmarts, Targets, and Costcos indicates how ethnically aware the market has become and the significant impact on American cuisine.

"My philosophy for running my stores is that, even though the name is Cub Foods, I'm a neighborhood grocer," says Keith Wyche, President and CEO of Cub Foods. "Each neighborhood is different. One of the things I did in this role was to give each of my store directors a demographic breakdown of who is in a two-mile radius—their income and ethnic breakdown. That's the first step in helping understand everything, beginning with hiring decisions. Because if you're in a community heavily populated with Hmong, you want to have someone there who can relate to Hmong people and who can tell you what they like and don't like."

Whether working in a multi-national organization like Halliburton or with a neighborhood grocery mindset like Cub Foods, companies today must have a global mindset. The business benefit is two-fold: *meeting* the needs of emerging markets and *growing* the demand for new products among existing markets. Brilliant! And chances are, the most enlightened brands found the seeds of innovation and customization from insights gleaned internally through employee input.

Endnotes

1. http://www.pwc.com/gx/en/world-2050/pdf/world2050emergin-geconomies.pdf.

2. Forbes Insights, "Global Diversity and Inclusion, Fostering Innovation through a Diverse Workforce." July 13, 2011.

3. "This is Generation Flux: Meet The Pioneers of The New (And Chaotic) Frontier of Business." See http://www.fastcompany.com/magazine/162/generation-flux-future-of-business.

4. PricewaterhouseCoopers' 9th Annual Global CEO Survey. 2006 (All respondents except Brazil, Russia, India, and China).

3

The War for Talent . . .
Gen Y As the Linchpin

My job is to bring in the best talent. I call it 'inclusive diversity,' meaning it is everyone, not just people of color and women. It includes white men. The question is, 'Who is the next up and comer?' I bring the best, brightest, and most diverse to the pool of candidates to organizations.

Michael Reid,
Managing Partner,
Boyden Global Executive Search

If you take diversity back to its original roots of diversity of thought—you want those ideas, you want those Gen X and Gen Y ideas.

Keith Wyche,
President and CEO,
Cub Foods

There's an interesting disconnect taking place in the U.S. today. Despite an unemployment rate that hovered around nine percent at the end of 2011, many companies lament that they are unable to find the qualified staff they need to fill key spots. How can this be? If you dig a little deeper, it's easy to see that the situation isn't so mysterious after all—it simply reflects the critical difference between the concepts of "talent" and "labor force."[1]

Talent represents the subset of the labor force that has the education and critical thinking skills to meet the evolving needs of employers. We may have an abundant supply of labor, but converting labor into talent is the key challenge and begs the million-dollar question: where are your new employees going to come from?

A CHANGING WORKFORCE

Between 2002–2012, the U.S. population over the age of fifty-five will grow forty-nine percent, while the population under age fifty-five will increase only five percent. According to the Federal Interagency Forum on Child and Family Statistics, the proportion of the American population made up of children aged zero to seventeen has fallen steadily from thirty-six percent in 1966 to 24.3 percent in 2009.[2]

That trend is projected to continue until at least 2050, when that age group is expected to make up only 23.1 percent of the total American population.

The first wave of the Baby Boomer generation turned sixty-two in 2008. The number of Boomers turning sixty-two will continue to grow, peaking in 2022 at a level more than sixty percent above the 2007 level. The aging of the nation will affect our labor markets and the demand for privately and publicly provided services.

It will also reduce the number of candidates available to organizations and will result in a workforce shortage.

Gen Y will represent the vast bulk of highly relevant and employable available "talent." Be prepared for "the Entitlement Age." In fact, it has already begun. Interestingly, predominantly white boomers will be watching for their entitlement benefits while members of Gen Y will be looking for their seat at the boardroom table.

Today, according to McKinsey,[3] forty-eight million of the more than 137 million U.S. workers are knowledge workers. About seventy percent of all U.S. jobs created since 1998—about 4.5 million jobs—require conceptual skills, note Jeanne Meister and Karie Willyerd in *The 2020 Workplace.*[4] These knowledge workers are crucial to a company's bottom line. In any organization, two things drive results: bringing in more revenue and saving money, both of which depend to a large extent on maintaining a robust pool of talented knowledge workers.

At the same time that we are seeing growth at the top end of the age range for employees, we will begin to see a significant growth in the number of non-white employees on the younger end of the age scale. As Ron Brownstein, a political correspondent with Atlantic Media pointed out in an NPR interview in 2011, almost forty-seven percent of the population in the U.S. under age eighteen is non-white. Our youth population will be "majority minority" by the end of this decade, he says. Contrast that to the aging Baby Boomer population.

In addition, one of the fastest growing demographic groups in the U.S. consists of those who self-identify as belonging to more than one ethnic group, e.g., Asian and Latino, or Latino and Black. As the number of interracial marriages continues to grow, this group will continue to be part of the workforce landscape. What does it mean for American businesses?

In one decade, the under eighteen demographic will begin to represent your workforce. It will begin to represent your customers. These will be people once considered "minorities." But guess what? They will no longer be the minority. An amalgamation of people from different demographic and cultural backgrounds, they will represent the majority.

A DEARTH OF TALENT

The sobering fact is that younger workers' numbers will be insufficient to replace their retiring colleagues, and their educational levels will likewise be in sharp contrast. While the jobs of the future require more education, the U.S. is struggling with excessive high school dropout rates. One sobering statistic reveals that twenty-five percent of our students—and almost forty percent of our black and Hispanic students—fail to graduate high school on time.[5]

The highest demographic growth occurs among the least educated populations at a time when the Bureau of Labor Statistics indicates, that between 2008-2018, more than half the new jobs created will be in professional and service-related occupations where postsecondary degrees are generally required. As minority students become a larger percentage of the population, their lower graduation rates will impact the availability of skilled, knowledge workers across all industries.

Where will the talent come from to fill the positions that require expertise and talent commensurate with a college education? Consider the changes in the following chart.

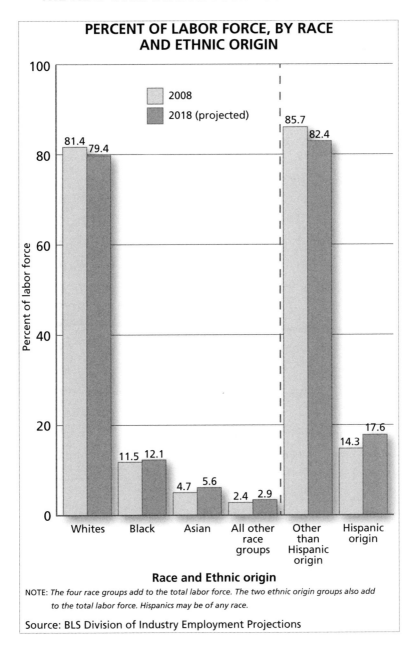

PERCENT OF LABOR FORCE, BY RACE AND ETHNIC ORIGIN

Legend:
- 2008
- 2018 (projected)

Whites: 81.4, 79.4
Black: 11.5, 12.1
Asian: 4.7, 5.6
All other race groups: 2.4, 2.9
Other than Hispanic origin: 85.7, 82.4
Hispanic origin: 14.3, 17.6

Y-axis: Percent of labor force
X-axis: Race and Ethnic origin

NOTE: *The four race groups add to the total labor force. The two ethnic origin groups also add to the total labor force. Hispanics may be of any race.*

Source: BLS Division of Industry Employment Projections

With the significant increases in Latinos, Asian-Americans, African Americans, and other ethnic groups, we might naturally expect the jobs to be filled by these emerging populations. Yet as the previous chart shows, in spite of the rapid growth of the non-white population referenced in Chapter 1, whites are projected to still represent 79.4 percent of the labor force even as late as 2018. At this rate, how will we make the gains necessary to reflect our emerging consumer base here and abroad?[6]

A slightly differing opinion about the makeup of the work-force is in *The 2020 Workplace*. Jeanne Meister and Karie Willyerd point to David A. Thomas and John J. Gabarro's book, *Breaking Through: The Making of Minority Executives in Corporate America*, and note that minority workers will make up close to forty percent of the U.S. workforce by 2020, yet more than fifty percent of all executive-level positions in the United States will continue to be held by white males.[7]

Women will also find themselves excluded from the executive suite. In 2007, women made up forty percent of the three billion people employed worldwide but held only twenty-four percent of senior management positions. To date, only 16.1 percent of corporate board seats in the United States are held by women[8]—this despite stronger financial performance among companies that have female board members.[9]

While the labor force will grow in both number and diversity, this growth will not be reflected in the talent available to meet organizations' rapidly emerging needs to address marketplace and consumer shifts in demand as well as increasing global competition. Available talent will be at a premium and highly sought after. The heightened war for talent means that organizations must consider ways in which they can position their organizations as great places to work—places where all input and insights will be valued.

THE NOTABLE IMPACT OF GEN Y

For the first time, four generations are represented in the workforce, including Boomers who will eventually be retiring en masse.

At no time in American history have so many different generations with such a diversity of world views and work philosophies been asked to team up and work together. Organizations that are generationally skilled value the differences between people and look at differences as strengths. Generationally balanced work groups respect and learn from yesterday's experiences, they understand today's pressures and needs and believe that tomorrow will be different still. Yet generational gaps, assumptions, and the use of stereotypes can get in the way of what could otherwise be great working relationships.

As employers continue to respond to changing age demographics, they should pay particular attention to the characteristics and needs of Gen Y. Why focus on Gen Y? Because this group represents such a significant percentage of the overall population.

Gen Y comprises over twenty-seven percent of the American population and nearly twenty-five percent of the American workforce today. These individuals, now aged eleven to thirty,[10] will comprise over fifty percent of the workforce by 2020.[11]

They are a force to be reckoned with, and as Boomers eventually leave the workforce, the Gen Y generations will not only replace them, they will in fact change the world.

While there are numerous differences between Gen Y and their predecessors in the Baby Boomer generation, four differences deserve a closer look:

1. Gen Y is more comfortable with technology.
2. They have never seen loyalty to a corporate culture pay off for their parents.
3. They tend to have greater comfort and familiarity with different ethnic groups.
4. They have limited patience with the status quo, much like Boomers who wanted to change the world.

Let's have a look at these four things in more detail.

1. Gen Y is more technologically savvy. Members of Gen Y have grown up with more technology than any other generation. As a consequence, their comfort with technology is key to their adaptability and collaborative work style. This group grew up with technology and social media and has a strong capacity to work with and leverage the currency of a knowledge-based global economy. If one platform or the latest "app" doesn't work, they try something else until they find a solution that meets their needs.

They are sometimes referred to as "technology natives," in contrast with older generations who often struggle to adapt to the new workplace tools that Gen Y takes for granted and demands.

2. Gen Y has never seen loyalty to a company pay off. As the war for talent heats up, employers and managers in older generations will have to accommodate this much sought-after cohort of employees. In many ways, Gen Y represents a significant change in personality from previous generations in the workforce. Gen Y is a generation with a sense of entitlement and interviews potential employers as much as they are interviewed themselves. They place a lot of value on maintaining a strong work-life balance.

While other generations saw work as an obligation or the defining element of their adult lives, Gen Y is much more likely to see a job as a means to an end and to have no problem leaving jobs they find unfulfilling. They are much more likely to hop from job to job than their elders. As the following chart shows, only 42 percent of young workers say it is likely they will stay at their current jobs for the rest of their working lives. This is very low compared to older generations. For example, sixty-two percent of Gen Xers say it is very likely they will stay at their current jobs, while eighty-four percent of Baby Boomers plan to stay put for the rest of their working lives.[12]

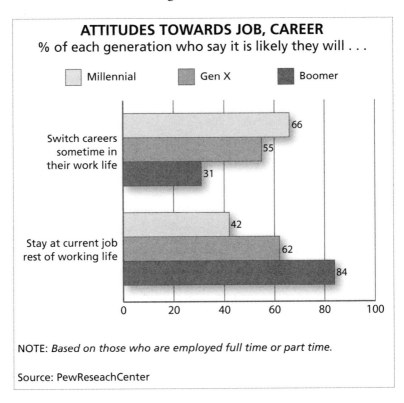

ATTITUDES TOWARDS JOB, CAREER
% of each generation who say it is likely they will . . .

- Millennial
- Gen X
- Boomer

Switch careers sometime in their work life
- 66
- 55
- 31

Stay at current job rest of working life
- 42
- 62
- 84

NOTE: *Based on those who are employed full time or part time.*

Source: PewReseachCenter

3. Gen Y is more comfortable with diverse ethnic groups. Gen Y's daily use of email, texting, and social networks is expected to follow them to the workplace and has made Gen Y an extremely social and interconnected group. This means they are not only more comfortable collaborating with coworkers virtually and in person but also that their social interactions aren't bound by geography. They are much more likely to be familiar with diverse and distant groups and cultures.

Additionally, Gen Y is much more ethnically and racially diverse than previous generations. White people make up only around sixty percent of this generation, with roughly twenty percent being identified as Hispanic. The growing competition for Gen Y employees in the workforce and this group's diversity means that companies will have to be increasingly willing and able to create diverse and inclusive organizations.

4. Gen Y has limited patience with the status quo. Members of Gen Y have grown up being encouraged by their parents not to take the world at face value. They have learned to question virtually everything and are sometimes called—somewhat pejoratively—"Generation Why."[13] This group is always looking for new ways to approach business as usual and isn't satisfied with answers like "Because that's the way it's always been done."

Many in older generations might look at this willingness to challenge the status quo as a lack of respect for authority or a know-it-all approach to professional life, but much of this willingness to challenge business as usual stems from the fact that members of Gen Y have grown up in a world of constant technological and societal change. They realize that doing things the way they have always been done simply won't continue to work.

All these characteristics mean that Gen Y will increasingly drive a whole new way of doing business, one that embraces new technologies, flexibility, and adaptability, and one that has limited respect for boundaries.

Endnotes

1. *The War for Talent: Myths and Reality.* The Korn/Ferry International Institute, 2008.

2. "POP2 Children As a Percentage of the Population." Federal Interagency Forum on Child and Family Statistics, 2011. See http://www.childstats.gov/americaschildren/tables/pop2.asp?popup=true.

3. "The Next Revolution in Interactions." Bradford C. Johnson, James M. Manyika, and Lareina Yee. *McKinsey Quarterly* 4 (2005), 25.

4. *The 2020 Workplace.* Jeanne C. Meister and Karie Willyerd. New York: Harper Collins, 2010.

5. http://nces.ed.gov/pubsearch/pubsinfo.asp?pubid=2010341.

6. "Employment Outlook: 2008-18." Bureau of Labor Statistics Monthly Labor Review, November 2009.

7. *The 2020 Workplace.* Jeanne C. Meister and Karie Willyerd. New York: Harper Collins, 2010.

8. "Women on Boards." Catalyst, 2011.

9. "The Bottom Line: Corporate Performance and Women's Representation on Boards." Catalyst, 2007.

10. "Generations in the Workplace in the United States and Canada." Catalyst, 2011.

11. "Generational Preferences: A Glimpse into the Future Office." Knoll Workplace Research, 2010.

12. "Millennials: A Portrait of Generation Next." Pew Research Center, Feb. 2010.

13. "Perception Versus Reality: 10 Truths about the Generation Y Workforce." Randall S. Hansen, Ph.D.

4
Diversity Fatigue

When I began my career in the mid '80s it was called diversity—there was no inclusion. It was really very much about making minorities and women a part of the corporate fabric. I think it was right for the times because it was still in its infancy. Unfortunately, what I've seen in the last twenty years is lots of companies that have never really gotten beyond the idea of focusing on gender and race.

Kim Koonce,
HR Executive,
formerly of Pepsico and Energy Future Holdings

Organizations for many years saw diversity as compliance. If you only focus on the numbers, leaders can feel beaten up or discouraged with the lack of progress. I believe, if you focus on changing the workplace to create a more inclusive environment, you will begin to see change that is sustainable.

Clydie Douglass,
Director Diversity and Inclusion,
3M

It's a real paradox that, at a time when the greatest changes are happening in the workforce and emerging markets, a fatigue has set in in the diversity arena. Historically, the focus on diversity has been driven by political, legal, and moral issues. Diversity gained momentum in the 1960s to level the playing field for people of color and women. It was considered "the right thing to do."

Over the last half century, we have seen increasing gains in workplace diversity starting with President Kennedy's signing of Executive Order 10925 in 1961, when we first saw the term "affirmative action." That was over fifty years ago, and it led to the passage of the Civil Rights Act in 1964.

Meanwhile, organizations that embraced "diversity work" seemed to focus on hiring women and people of color or focused on training. Over time, these good intentions to create a more ethnically and racially diverse workforce began to focus on "getting representation" and educating people about differences. This has been a numbers game that in many cases lacked a clear business linkage. Corporate America has been spinning its wheels for decades, attempting to influence change by focusing on the numbers, and it hasn't worked.

"Throw the diversity stuff out," urges Kelly Elkin, International Commercial Banker, formerly of Norwest, U.S. Bank, and Bremer. "Focus on inclusion. Do we really want people who are engaged? Do we really want to hear their ideas? Once you start including people, that's naturally going to attract diverse populations because people who feel included are going to share their ideas." She adds, "I think if you focus on the inclusion first, the diversity will come."

To date, training has been a primary driver to address diversity awareness needs within organizations. In implementing this training, many organizations have taken a personal, internalized approach. There are academic approaches that determine how biased we are and categorize us as employees as a way of determining organizational readiness. But where is the business linkage? Where are the resulting behaviors that impact the business identified? How do we hold people accountable?

Learning should be a result of a current state analysis and a component within a business strategy. What are the other training drivers that need to shift within organizations?

- Companies must move from diversity management alone to creating a culture of inclusion.
- Companies must extend learning beyond just senior leaders and implement an enterprise-wide approach with methodology appropriate for all levels of the organization.
- Companies must make the business linkage, including engagement, productivity, innovation, and retention.
- Companies must urge inclusion and diversity training efforts that are more than a "dip and done" (where training happens every three to seven years but with no accountability or performance plan in between).
- Companies must create a systematic accelerated "Learning over Time®" strategy using metrics and accountability.
- Companies must be strategic; inclusion and diversity training efforts must move past awareness and link back to business behaviors in the workplace.
- Companies must measure the transfer of behaviors back to the workplace to ensure the effectiveness of the training.
- Companies must hold people accountable.

It's important to note that the language in this important space has morphed over time, as the following example shows:

In the first decade of the new millennium, many initiatives floundered due to tough economic times, so the focus needs to be on the business drivers in the chart above. Now, in the second decade of the twenty-first century, we are experiencing a muted call to action on diversity and facing many of the same issues that organizations, and their employees and customers, have faced for decades. To really impact change, our focus needs to be on connecting the dots to the business and moving past representation metrics to a culture of inclusion.

"We're really trying to stay away from seeing it as an initiative," says Shanequa Williams, Human Capital Business Partner at Select Comfort Corporation. "We're really at the place where we're trying to figure out how we can create a strategy that's going to be sustainable—one that will stand the test of time; one that will yield business results."

That's exactly what organizations need to be focused on, but too many are simply "giving up." While many organizations are making great strides, many more have shifted away from diversity. They go through the motions to meet the minimum requirements, but they have not fully integrated the business potential that inclusion could yield for them, for their employees, for their customers, and ultimately, for their stakeholders.

Then there are those who say we've moved beyond the need for these discussions. Because a president of color is now in the White House, some would have us believe our work is complete. But is it? Pay inequities and disparities still exist among certain groups, and the gaps haven't narrowed by much. For example in 2010, the median weekly earnings of full-time Hispanic wage and salary workers was $535.00, while wages for whites were $765.00.[1] Yet, while we continue to see disparities based on race, we are seeing signs of progress in statistics that show us that more women than men are now graduating and getting college degrees, masters degrees, and doctorates.[2]

These may be signs of progress, but economic disparities are greater than ever, and a far greater number of people feel disenfranchised. The economic gap continues to grow, and the middle class is disappearing. It now takes two incomes for young people to even approach the lifestyles their parents had. This goes beyond race and gender.

It's not that race and gender aren't still important, but in today's world of the new business normal, the conversations have become much more complex and nuanced. InclusionINC, my consulting firm, has created assessments to determine where the breakdowns occur, what stands in the way of being fully engaged, and what it takes to ensure employees feel included and can be most innovative and productive. From data collected from this assessment work with more than 310,000 U.S.

employees across multiple industries, primarily in the corporate environment, I have found that breakdowns occur primarily because of five key factors:

1. This is the first time in U.S. history in which we have four generations in the workplace.
2. Cross-cultural issues are emerging whether you're dealing with a global colleague or someone from your own office.
3. Employee engagement and productivity are driven by an organization's understanding that everyone contributes to the business success.
4. Innovation is driven by an organization's ability to effectively include all perspectives.
5. Technology has significantly changed how individuals communicate; inclusive communication is becoming even more critically important for innovation.

Many businesses are ill-prepared to recognize, let alone address, these factors because of the complexities involved.

The result? Diversity fatigue, and the sense that all these efforts, however well-intentioned, are simply not relevant to business. Ultimately, diversity fatigue leads to resignation, and when times get tough, the programs and people deemed non-essential are cut. Sadly, as mentioned in the Foreword of this book, Corporate America has historically tended to see diversity as something that's "the right thing to do" but not necessarily something it "needs to do" as a business driver. Most organizations still have difficulty recognizing that the diversity of their workforce and the mobilization of diverse workers is central to tapping the growth in new and emerging markets.

Today, we need to do something different. We need to move from a focus on diversity to a focus on inclusion and diversity or, simply, a focus on inclusion. Not because it's the "right thing to do" but because it is a business imperative. A war for talent is looming, and businesses that wish to succeed in an environment facing such seismic shifts must focus on strategies designed to attract, retain, and generate input and innovative ideas from a changing, but also shrinking, talent base.

Importantly, notes Kim Koonce, HR Executive, formerly of Pepsico and Energy Future Holdings, the shift from diversity to inclusion impacts all of us. She says, "I think the recent changes are positive and forward-moving in that it's now turning the dial to another level. There's this collective sigh of relief from every white man under forty who says, 'Oh, good, so this isn't going to be about me walking on eggshells and feeling I'm not part of the dialogue, or that I'm the problem.' Now they're actually going to be part of the solution. I think that's the biggest change that is going to be the most productive."

Endnotes

1. "Hispanics Earn Less Than Whites, African-Americans." Fox News, April 1, 2011.

2. "Why Are More Women Than Men Going to College?" Palash R. Ghosh. *International Business Times.*

5

The Need
for Innovation

Today, it is customer-driven marketing in which the customer makes the decisions about what they want. In order to gain that kind of customer insight, you've got to have a truly diverse workforce.

Donald Fan,
Senior Director, Global Office of Diversity,
Walmart

You really don't know where a good idea may come from. If you alienate part of an organization, you can miss a good idea.

Clarence Nunn,
President and CEO,
GE Capital Fleet Services

In the modern global economy, companies can't afford to stand still and rest on their laurels. What may once have been a game-changing business strategy or novel invention can be copied or made obsolete in an instant by competitors from any corner of the globe. To maintain a competitive advantage and continue to be profitable, businesses need to be able to innovate. In other words, "What got you here won't get you there."

So what does "innovation" actually mean? The term suggests cutting-edge technological advancements and futuristic inventions. However, innovation is much more than the process of scientific invention. While these types of breakthroughs certainly represent the possible end results of innovation, a complete definition also includes creativity, insight, and challenging traditional ways of thinking and operating.

A European Union study defined innovation as "the generation and introduction of new ideas, which lead to the development of new products and services, processes, and systems in all areas of business activity."[1]

In other words, innovation is both the idea and the outcome. It's not enough to simply think of new ideas; companies must generate some profitable use or benefit from them.

Why is innovation so critical for modern companies? It's no secret that we live and work in an increasingly global economy. As your business is exposed to more and more markets, you will need to constantly find new ways to cater to the changing and diverse needs of those markets and to compete with businesses that may already be capitalizing on the innovation. One way to do this is to find innovative new ways to meet the needs of a variety of cultures and tastes. Recall the regionalized variations that companies like Coca-Cola, McDonald's, and Nabisco have used to tap into their diverse markets. These subtle, market-specific variations are great examples of how these companies have been innovative as they've attempted to expand the reach of their products to a global environment.

Ultimately, innovation comes from people. As Clydie Douglass, Director Diversity and Inclusion at 3M, notes, "Many studies have been done showing that a team of people who are very similar isn't as creative or as effective as a team that has a mix of experiences, background, and education. If you encourage the input of the person who has a different perspective or doesn't follow the 'groupthink,' you will have a stronger outcome."

Kelly Elkin, International Commercial Banker, formerly of Norwest, U.S. Bank, and Bremer, agrees: "Inclusion equals positive bottom line results. Your next product, your next service, your next efficiency is going to come from someone within your organization who is perhaps not in a management or leadership role. But, because management or leadership has taken the time to engage that individual or group of individuals who have diverse backgrounds, you now have come up with the best new product or service or back office efficiency, which equals an improved bottom line."

Certainly, innovation can lead to significant competitive advantage that creates something different or better than what the competition has to offer. Competitive advantage allows companies to outperform others in terms of market share, cost savings, or revenue generation. An innovative new production technique, for example, can allow a company to produce its products more cost effectively than its major competitors, helping it send more of its revenue to the bottom line. But competitive advantages do not last forever.

The Model T was a great thing in its time. So were VHS tapes and newspapers. But the world continues to change around us, and we need to change with it. Companies that create a culture of innovation and consistently capitalize on new ideas and ways of thinking can stay ahead of the competition and ahead of changing needs among the markets they serve.

Let's consider some of the recent major impacts on companies that failed to innovate quickly enough to address emerging markets and the massive impacts of new technology.

Blockbuster filed for bankruptcy in 2010 with a plan to restructure through major cost-cutting efforts (a.k.a. layoffs—the company shut down a third of its 4,500 U.S. sites in 2009). The once-profitable and, yes, innovative company failed to continue to innovate in the face of emerging competition and new delivery models through services like Netflix and Redbox.[2] In 2009, General Motors Company (GM) filed for and emerged from Chapter 11 bankruptcy—the largest bankruptcy filing of a U.S. industrial company.[3] The biggest example of an entire industry's failure to respond to changing market needs and competitive pressures, GM is a good example of an old "command and control" style company that likely failed to recognize the value represented through the brainpower of its more than 200,000 employees. Time will tell whether GM has learned through its experiences.

In the summer of 2011, Borders, the second-largest U.S. bookstore chain, was forced to liquidate its stores, impacting about 11,000 employees. In a *Wall Street Journal* article, Borders' president Mike Edwards said, ". . . the head winds we have been facing for quite some time, including the rapidly changing book industry, [electronic reader] revolution, and turbulent economy, have brought us to where we are now."[4] Could Borders have benefitted from more innovative thinking about new marketing and delivery methods? Who knows?

With these companies and many others, numerous impacts ultimately mark their demise. But other companies that are renowned for capturing the hearts and minds of their employees and cultivating their ideas seem to thrive even in a turbulent economy marked by disruptive technologies and increasing competition. They do things differently. They stimulate change. They remain attuned to what people are thinking—not just their employees but also their markets. And they adjust their practices, and sometimes even their products, to address these changing needs.

They recognize that the sum of the parts can be greater than the whole. Donald Fan, Senior Director, Global Office of Diversity at Walmart, stresses that decision-making is not a "binary mindset." It's not an issue of either/or, right/wrong. Too often, he says, when presented with two options, the tendency is to select one because it's "better than the other, versus having a more integrative way of thinking." He explains, "I say, 'How can I use the strengths and advantages of each of these solutions and then come up with a *third solution that best addresses the true issues or dilemmas?*'"

The innovative companies get it. Think Apple. Think Twitter. Think Facebook. They top the list of *Fast Company's* most innovative companies in 2011. That makes sense; they're technology companies. And at number four is Nissan for "creating the Leaf, the first mass-market, all-electric car." This is a pretty amazing accomplishment, considering the volatility of the auto industry in the last decade. Nissan has had its ups and downs, but it has responded successfully to significant challenges, competitive pressures, and changing marketing dynamics.[5]

That's innovation. It's the kind of innovation that comes from remaining aware of and responding to the myriad changes that impact companies every day. That means recognizing that it's not just the people at the top of the organization who have all the great ideas. It means valuing the input and perspective of each and every member of the organization—recognizing that you never know where that next great insight or idea may come from. It means seeking out diverse opinions to make sure your organization isn't just responding to one narrow niche in the market but is prepared to hear and address multiple perspectives from multiple sources.

"It has to do with business," says Kim Koonce, HR Executive, formerly of Pepsico and Energy Future Holdings. "It has to do with people learning to be open and to accept a variety of people and their thoughts and ideas." She gives an example of a company she worked at where the longest-tenured people were the most valued. "So, your ideas and your thoughts were less valid than theirs," she recalls. "It was discrimination; it just wasn't illegal. So, for me, the business did not benefit from my abilities because I was in many ways excluded from conversations and my value wasn't maximized." As Clarence Nunn said at the beginning this chapter, "If you alienate part of an organization, you can miss a good idea."

Resolve not to miss *any* good ideas. Embrace innovation by embracing the voices of your employees and customers—*all* of their voices.

Endnotes

1. "Diversity and Innovation: A Business Opportunity for All." European Commission, 2009.

2. http://money.cnn.com/2010/09/23/news/companies/blockbuster_bankruptcy/index.htm.

3. http://www.instantshift.com/2010/02/03/22-largest-bankruptcies-in-world-history/.

4. http://online.wsj.com/article/SB10001424052702303661904576454353768550280.html.

5. http://bx.businessweek.com/apple/view?url=http%3A%2F%2Fwww.fastcompany.com%2Fmost-innovative-companies%2F2011%2F.

6
On to Inclusion

I call inclusion the engine that drives diversity. That's the base to me. I'm trying to make Halliburton a more inclusive place first, not a more diverse organization. I feel that if you make it inclusive, diversity will come.

Cindy Bigner,
Director, Global Diversity and Inclusion,
Halliburton

For some organizations, diversity was just the latest iteration of Affirmative Action and so they had to grow beyond that. Conversely, there are organizations that kind of get it but yet have not really figured out that it takes more than hiring somebody and making them a VP of diversity.

Keith Wyche,
President and CEO,
Cub Foods

While many organizations are making efforts to promote diversity strategies, they often come up short. In the last chapter, I discussed the concept of "diversity fatigue." Many organizations are sick of hearing about how they should or must make their companies more diverse by hiring more women, hiring more people of color, and opening up the ranks of upper management to underrepresented groups.

To some extent, these complaints are valid, since organizations have historically counted women and people of color at all levels of the organization as a primary approach to incorporating diversity.

STOP COUNTING, START INCLUDING

Inclusion calls us to action. It's not limited to representation metrics as the primary driver. That focus serves to lead organizations into a talent acquisition frenzy. It's not that there's anything wrong with recruiting, but I've seen organizations spend literally tens of thousands of dollars to participate in recruiting events just to, essentially, check a box. Their intent may be noble, but their thinking is limited. A company may hire the greatest talent, but if there isn't a culture of inclusion, that talent will move on.

While the language of diversity was a way to address dealing with a broad range of differences, the focus turned primarily on talent acquisition of women and people of color. The impact of this narrowing focus was:

- It did *not* make the strong business link that was required to be mission critical.
- Diversity seemed to be driven by representation metrics.

- Diversity was seen as a U.S. phenomenon only and didn't seem relevant globally.
- It didn't include everyone.

Today, I continue to see confusion in the language of inclusion associated with diversity. I see the term "inclusion" used interchangeably with "diversity." Let me emphasize what I hope by now is obvious: *these terms are not interchangeable!*

Let's look at the definitions of inclusion and diversity.

Diversity—(noun). Describes the differences between people.

Diversity is essentially all the ways in which we differ from one another. Primary dimensions of diversity include age, gender, race, ethnicity, sexual orientation, and physical abilities/qualities. These dimensions of diversity are generally obvious and essentially unchangeable, and they can have a powerful effect on an individual's opportunities.

Diversity also includes dimensions such as socioeconomics, thinking style, personality, educational level, values, religious beliefs, work style, and occupation.

Inclusion—(a call to action). Includes everyone's voice and talents.

Inclusion means being open to a variety of ideas, knowledge, perspectives, approaches, and styles from everyone, ensuring that everyone is allowed to bring their best to the workplace to maximize business success.

TYING INNOVATION TO INCLUSION AND DIVERSITY

Chapter 5 established the importance of innovation, but what does that have to do with inclusion and diversity? While many business leaders might not immediately connect these concepts, the reality is that inclusion and diversity are important elements in creating an innovative culture. Innovation involves constantly finding new ways to attack problems and looking beyond traditional ways of producing and marketing products and services. Hiring a diverse workforce and then *including* the perspectives of all members of that diverse workforce is a natural and proven way to yield innovative ideas.

After all, diversity doesn't just mean having a sprinkling of employees from a variety of racial or ethnic groups in your organization. Diversity means hiring people from a variety of age, socio-economic, geographic, religious, educational, and experiential backgrounds as well as maintaining diversity in terms of racial, ethnic, and gender groups because it makes sense for the business. While maintaining diversity is certainly an important element in creating an inclusive workplace, diversity alone is not enough.

Inclusion goes beyond simply having a diverse pool of employees. It's about engaging those employees so they become active contributors in the organization, coming up with great ideas and participating in decision-making. If you put a group of people with similar backgrounds in a room together and ask them to solve a problem, they're likely to come up with very similar ideas and they're even more likely to agree with each other. This is because "groupthink" doesn't generally lead to innovative ideas.

But get a group of people from different backgrounds together and they're likely to look at problems and opportunities in very different ways, magnifying the creativity of the entire group. That can be a great thing!

Challenging accepted patterns of thinking is an important element of innovation. If people in your organization tend to make comments like, "Well, that's the way we've always done it here," chances are there's not a lot of outside-the-box thinking going on. On the other hand, creating an inclusive environment and welcoming opposing points of view and challenges to the status quo allows organizations, the business community, and society in general to benefit.

Employees will be able to tap into diverse backgrounds; drawing upon a variety of personal, professional, and educational experiences. That will lend to brainstorming fresh ideas and new ways of looking at things.

Ultimately, innovation is a product of an organization's human capital. If an organization is composed of a homogeneous labor pool with similar backgrounds and experiences, the organization can expect uniform thought processes and solutions. To generate new and different ideas, companies must be proactive and intentional about including as many diverse viewpoints as possible.

YES, RECRUIT THEM— BUT YOU HAVE TO KEEP THEM!

Yet recruitment is only part of the equation. If, as the CEO of an organization, I'm harping about how we don't hire enough women and people of color but I'm not linking that recruitment strategy to the business, these efforts are not going to work. I may be able to recruit from specific groups, but will I be able to keep those I hire? Or will I ultimately be forced to conclude that "They just didn't work out"?

To move toward the creation of a culture of inclusion that will have meaningful and measurable impacts on the bottom line, companies need to:

- Move past compliance as motivation
- Link their efforts to the business plan
- Focus on the bottom line
- Emphasize inclusion as a culture change
- Focus on the value of each individual
- View employees as "assets" (i.e., intellectual capital)

Inclusion is about taking action to get everybody's voice heard because that's what will drive business performance. Everybody means *everybody*. Yes, it means women and people of color, but it also means men and Caucasians. It means employees who are Republicans and employees who are Democrats as well as employees who are Muslim, Christian, and Atheist. It means employees who are Traditionalists (those born between 1900–1945) and employees who represent Gen Y.

Clydie Douglass, Director Diversity and Inclusion at 3M, says, "Organizations for many years saw diversity as compliance (i.e., hire more of xxx). Today, organizations are realizing that diversity includes all the ways we are unique, but inclusion is how we leverage those unique characteristics to drive innovation and growth for both our businesses and our employees."

TOWARD A CULTURE OF INCLUSION

The shift from focusing on diversity to focusing on inclusion is in process. No specific date or year highlights when it started because this shift has been more evolutionary than revolutionary.

Even our "old conversations" with CEOs and other business leaders included an element of inclusion. When we had these conversations in the past, we talked about promoting a welcoming, respectful workplace. That is really a reflection of inclusion—we just hadn't put a label on it yet. And, as we've discussed, because the focus tended to be on women and people of color, we were inadvertently being *exclusionary.*

Most important, that exclusion (whether it's African American women or Caucasian men being excluded) impacts the business, and that's what it's all about. Shouldn't inclusion be for everyone?® Inclusion has to be looked at as a business strategy, because that's what it really is. It will improve your business. It will make you more competitive. It will boost your bottom line.

The data we gathered in our customized InclusionINC inclusion and diversity assessment work of 310,000 employees throughout Corporate America has helped me define the business behaviors that reflect inclusion. And guess what? It's not rocket science. These are simple behaviors. For example, when we asked participants, "When do you feel most included?", the number one response was "When I'm asked my opinion" or "When they ask me how to make the change."

This doesn't have to be a big deal. Business behaviors that support inclusion don't have to involve ambitious rewards and recognition programs. These behaviors can be as simple as two powerful words: "Thank you."

Behaviors that support inclusion involve taking the time to listen—not just telling people what to do. When changes occur, behaviors that support inclusion involve giving people the rationale for why certain decisions have been made and, better yet, inviting their input as part of the decision-making process. Behaviors that support inclusion allow decision-making down to the associate or very junior level. These behaviors encourage involvement at every tier within the organization and from every individual in the organization.

Every individual. Every single individual. That's inclusion.

7

Inclusion Is the Solution to Employee Engagement

To keep a competitive advantage, everyone needs to not only have a voice but also to be heard.

Rebecca Robinson,
Office of Diversity and Inclusion,
3M

I think that as companies, it's important for people to feel like they have a voice because that's the only way they rally around a strategy. You have to create an environment where people feel they can't hide and where they believe they have a voice in the process.

Clarence Nunn,
President and CEO,
GE Capital Fleet Services

Not all organizations recognize the value of building a workforce of engaged employees. The stars get it—Zappos, Whole Foods, Google. The companies that make the "Best Places to Work" lists and find themselves inundated with applicants who are the best and the brightest.

What are these companies doing that others aren't? Why are some organizations getting it right while others continue to flounder with less-than-stellar business results? Why do so many organizations struggle to find and keep productive employees as well as retain their best customers? What are these organizations missing?

The answer is simple: a workplace culture of inclusion.

Inclusion provides key insights and behaviors that ensure connectivity to the complexity of the current global market. Inclusion is about encouraging people to share their best ideas. Inclusion means getting people to participate in reaching the best outcome for the organization. Inclusion is about getting everyone in the game to ensure their voices are heard to improve overall business success. Inclusion is the best practical solution for employee engagement.

Why has employee engagement become such a huge matter, and how does inclusion impact it? Let's start with defining employee engagement, which measures the level of connection employees feel toward their employer as demonstrated by their willingness and ability to help their company succeed, largely by providing discretionary effort on a sustained basis.[1]

Inclusion, as explained in Chapter 6, is an action word and means including everyone's voice and talents. It means being open to a variety of ideas, knowledge, perspectives, approaches, and styles. It means everyone is allowed to bring their best to the workplace to maximize business success.

Today, inclusion and employee engagement are inexorably linked because most employees are knowledge workers who create value through the synergy that results from the confluence of ideas and information.

Inclusive organizations recognize that they need input from *everybody* to help drive business decisions and productivity. Truck drivers as well as sales managers have knowledge to share; facility staff as well as accounting staff can provide valid perspectives to improve business processes and results.

Kim Koonce, HR Executive, formerly of Pepsico and Energy Future Holdings, notes that, "I have never found an employee who, if at the end of the day they got to speak their mind and you listened to them, debated with them, looked at them and said, 'I hear what you are saying; this is the decision we're making and here is why . . .' didn't feel good that they got their moment to speak."

Even if your business is based in the U.S., you're not just competing with U.S. companies today. Everything is global— your employees, your markets, and your competition. Hearing and integrating ideas from all your employees is a key driver for success in this new global business normal.

Organizations bring in more revenue when they are appropriately focused on meeting the needs of customers, whoever and wherever they are. They bring in more revenue and contain costs when they are fully engaged with their stakeholders, which leads to creative and innovative solutions from their employees to meet customer needs and changing demands.

Clearly, your company's bottom line will benefit by generating new ideas and increasing productivity. Unfortunately, too many organizations spend too little time working on creating sustainable, engaging work environments in which people can participate.

"THEY'RE HUMAN CAPITAL, NOT CATTLE"[2]

The importance of employee engagement is also due in large part to the transformation of the workforce from laborers to knowledge workers. Years ago, employment relationships were relatively simple. An employer with valuable resources at his disposal would hire employees to use those resources—under the direction of the employer or his agents—to create something of value. The employee did as she was told. She had nothing to offer aside from her labor, and that labor was a commodity easily interchangeable with virtually any other worker. In short, "engagement" simply meant making sure an employee showed up to work and put sufficient effort into her job—basically doing what she was told.

Today, things are much different, and that has almost everything to do with the emergence of knowledge workers. As the VeraSage Institute has pointed out, "Knowledge workers are not like workers from the Industrial Revolution who were dependent on the employing organization providing the means of production (factories and machines). Today, knowledge workers themselves own the firm's means of production in their heads."[3]

Getting the most out of your organization therefore means getting the most out of your people. The 2006 World Bank study, "Where Is the Wealth of Nations?", found that seventy-five percent of the world's wealth resides in human capital. With so much value and productive capacity residing in a company's people, engagement absolutely has to be a top priority for any organization. Human capital is simply too valuable to waste.

What exactly is human capital? An early definition can be found in the namesake of the World Bank study just mentioned, Adam Smith's *The Wealth of Nations*. In this classic work of economics, Smith defines human capital as "the economic value of an employee's skill set, including knowledge and experience." Like a factory, human capital can be improved through investment, such as employee training or education.

Companies must come to grips with this new reality if they want to retain the best employees and, more importantly, take advantage of their most valuable resource: human capital. Among the organizations that capitalize on the value of the knowledge their employees possess is Google. Google provides its employees twenty percent of their time to work on projects that interest them. In this new era of knowledge workers, it doesn't make sense to hire smart people and then tell them what to do. When we hire smart people, we should let them tell *us* what to do, and tell us they do, through a variety of communication channels that literally allow them to be connected 24/7.

According to the International Data Corporation (IDC), "hyperconnected" professionals currently make up sixteen percent of the workforce and are expected to quickly increase to forty percent. These hyperconnected professionals are found in all countries but more so in Latin America and the Pacific region, according to the IDC. Not surprisingly, sixty percent of them are under the age of thirty-five.[4] A new phrase has even emerged to refer to the increasingly blurred line that exists between work and leisure time, "weisure time."[5] No doubt, social media has had a significant impact on the ability and the desire to stay connected at all hours of the day, blurring the lines between workplace and home.

Simultaneously, companies like Google focus on effectiveness rather than efficiency. They recognize that getting "more" out of employees may not be reflected in traditional productivity outputs but in future innovation—harder to measure but arguably more critical to the long-term sustainability of the organization. Knowledge work is defined by quality, not quantity, and the best way to get quality input is to engage employees, to make them *want* to contribute their best and most creative ideas. This kind of engagement requires abandoning the traditional top-down management approach and embracing the idea that knowledge workers are motivated more by a personal desire to succeed than by a fear of punishment.

Yet many individuals focused on making the numbers for Wall Street have somehow forgotten about the value of the people behind those numbers. In the radically changing workforce, engaging employees is important and far more complicated. As business leaders have been focused elsewhere, the nature and needs of the people who will fuel their future success have been changing. The old saying applies: "Adapt, migrate, mutate, or die."

Cindy Bigner, drawing on her role as Director of Global Diversity and Inclusion at Halliburton, has this to say: "Engagement and inclusion run hand in hand, but inclusion is the engine. And it's so cheap for companies to do. Once you train your employees what inclusion means, how it feels to be included, what it means to engage others, and show them what they get when they engage others, it's something you can't put a price on."

NOT THE TIME FOR PANIC

Before you start to panic, understand that there are some easy ways to engage your diverse workforce:

- **Share your strategy with your employees.** Let's say you're worried about increasing competition and the emergence of new technology and markets that might make your products obsolete. Have you told your employees, or do you figure they just need to punch in and punch out at the right time and work their part of the assembly line? Do you think, "What could they possibly have to offer me?" If so, you're thinking wrong. Sharing your strategy with employees not only gives them perspective about how their efforts fit into the big picture and drives organizational success, it increases the odds that they will share their unique insights and ideas with you.

- **Ask for their input.** Include them! If you rely entirely on a handful of managers and top executives to come up with great new ideas, you're missing out on the brain-power of the majority of your workplace. When making hiring decisions, most employers look for employees who are creative, intelligent, and insightful. Why hire people like that if you aren't going to ask for their input? These are the people on the ground, the ones who will implement any new strategy your organization pursues, the ones selling your products and services to your customers, the ones who have seen firsthand what works and what doesn't.

- **Listen and evaluate the idea, not the person presenting it.** What could that twenty-one-year-old business graduate possibly know about improving productivity or product quality? What could that sixty-two-year-old possibly know about technology? You might be surprised. Similarly, as your markets and customer base become more diverse, it is increasingly important to get input from all your employees. Don't you think your Hispanic employees might have some insights into the tastes of their friends, families, and communities? When you put up barriers in your mind as to the value of the input and opinions that employees have to offer, you're being exclusive. Your employees lose out, but guess what? So do you!

- **Act on what you determine to be the best course of action.** You can't take everyone's suggestions, and that's okay. Inclusion is first and foremost about making sure everyone gets a chance to be heard, even if their ideas aren't always used.

- **Provide feedback to your employees about why you did or did not take their suggestions.** Again, it's impossible and impractical to use everyone's suggestions, but your employees might think their ideas were particularly useful and may be confused if they aren't implemented. It's important to let them know specifically why one path was taken and not another. This will reassure employees that their ideas were truly considered and not just passed over. Additionally, this will benefit your organization by improving future input. If any employee's input is particularly helpful, let them know specifically how it contributed to the final decision and how it will help the company.

- **Thank your employees for being willing to contribute.** Think about times when you've contributed something to a brainstorming session or strategic planning effort. Did you feel like you received recognition or appreciation for your contribution? Too often, this is not the case. Simply stopping at an employee's desk and taking a few seconds to personally thank them can go a long way towards making them feel included and eager to contribute in the future. Let them know that even if their ideas aren't being used this time around, you feel they have a lot to offer and you look forward to getting their input in the future.

Hopefully you've noticed an important three-part theme resonating in all these suggestions: share, ask, listen. The key to creating an inclusive workplace is often as simple as being more effective at communicating. Even the most well-meaning workplace can seem exclusionary if there is poor communication. Taking the extra time to share new strategies with employees and simply asking what they think can go a long way toward making employees feel valued and engaged. And who knows, you might learn a thing or two in the process!

Endnotes

1. Towers Watson. See http://www.towerswatson.com/assets/pdf/629/ Manager-Recognition_Part1_WP_12-24-09.pdf.

2. VeraSage. See http://www.verasage.com/index.php/Community/ comments/human_capital_not_cattle.

3. Ibid.

4. IDC, "The Hyperconnected: Here They Come." See http://www2.nortel.com/go/news_detail.jsp?cat_id=-9742&oid=100240224&locale=en-US (accessed August 17, 2011).

5. "Welcome to the 'Weisure' Lifestyle," Thom Patterson, CNN.com, May 11, 2009. See www.cnn.com/2009/LIVING/worklife/05/11/ weisure/index.html (accessed August 17, 2011).

8
Inclusion Is the Solution to Retention

You can hire persons of color, you can hire men and women—that's great, you can 'mark the box.' But if you don't include them, if you don't have an inclusive environment, then what's the point? They're going to be unhappy; they're going to leave!

Kelly Elkin,
International Commercial Banker,
formerly of Norwest, U.S. Bank, and Bremer

The inclusion piece, in my mind, is the most important. I call it the engine that drives diversity. I can go out and hire diverse employees all day long, but if I'm not inclusive in my organization—if I don't include those diverse employees—forget it. They're not going to stay.

Cindy Bigner,
Director, Global Diversity and Inclusion,
Halliburton

According to Forbes, as many as seventy-five percent of an organization's top performers can be expected to leave within three years.[1]

In addition, because employers have increasingly been unable to demonstrate loyalty to their workers, employees have abandoned loyalty in return. While "job hopping" used to be considered a bad thing by the old guard, those who have multiple experiences at multiple companies are often highly valued today for their breadth of knowledge, their agility, and their broad insights. But while your biotechnology firm might be eager to hire a thirty-something with experience at four major competitors over the course of a brief career, you're likely *not* so eager to have your competitors picking off *your* bright staff members. With them, you'd likely want to see a longer tenure than two years.

Don't you long for the good old days, when things were simpler and people stayed forever? Well, sorry folks, but those days are long gone. According to the Bureau of Labor Statistics, the median job tenure for workers aged fifty-five to sixty-four was ten years in 2010. That's more than three times the median job tenure for workers aged twenty-five to thirty-four, which was 3.1 years. In fact in 2008, Experience, Inc. reported that seventy percent of Gen Y leave their first job within two years.

Turnover represents real costs to businesses. Ending an existing employment relationship, finding a replacement, and training that replacement can be a huge drain on your organization. Employee retention is essential for keeping your best and brightest, for keeping your HR costs down, and for minimizing knowledge loss.

RETENTION IN THE EVER-CHANGING WORKPLACE

Today we have four, soon to be five, generations in the workplace. This poses a unique issue for retaining your best talent. The key to keeping the best of the best in each generation is to understand the differences and strengths each generation brings to the table. If you understand what makes each generation feel engaged and included, you can be a successful leader of your multigenerational workforce. Generations differ in the way they communicate, in how they view their work, in how they receive feedback, and in what techniques they use to accomplish tasks. Here are some tips to help bridge the generational divide:

- Value diversity of thought
- Know whom you're talking to
- Learn to accept and appreciate everyone's perspective
- Discuss expectations right away
- Make everyone feel included
- Don't be put off by overt ambition
- Keep up with technology

The workforce is also more culturally diverse than ever before. Both on the local and global level, cultural differences can create conflicts in the workplace and lead to retention issues. Depending on their culture, employers and employees alike may have very different perceptions of time, feedback styles, hierarchies and many other everyday business tasks. Being aware of cultural differences and seeing those differences as strengths can help you retain the culturally diverse workforce that can give you an advantage over your competitors.

Creating Business Resource Groups (also known as Employee Resource Groups, Employee Networks, or Affinity Groups) can help make your diverse workforce feel more included. Such groups also allow individuals to share their experiences with others who may be having similar experiences and aid in achieving key business objectives.

For example, if your organization is trying to tap into the Chinese market, your Asian Business Resource Group should be included in that discussion since these individuals have a unique perspective that can help identify the culture and demands of that particular market. Now you not only have the competitive advantage over your competitors who have a room full of Americans trying to decide what the Chinese market might want but you've also made your employees feel like they truly belong at your organization by making this contribution.

Clarence Nunn, President and CEO of GE Capital Fleet Services, explains it this way: "It has to be part of your business strategy and you have to treat it like any other business process. That's the only way it becomes a part of the way you work because if your team says that a particular Affinity Group (AG) is not performing well, you probably don't have the right leaders of the AG. You have to ask yourself, 'Who's that lead? How is it being run? How does one of the successful AGs operate?' Have you gotten those two leadership teams together?"

RETAINING GEN Y . . . REALLY!

Let's get a couple things on the table right now. Gen Y is never going to "grow up" and be like the Baby Boomers. They are already grown up! Whereas Baby Boomers were likely to stay with one company for years and sometimes for entire careers, Gen Y (as dynamic and as creative as they are) is a far more flighty cohort. This generation knows it can easily transition between jobs and careers, and Gen Y places a huge value on work life balance. These folks don't want to be forced to abandon time with family and friends for a career. They work to live, rather than live to work, and they will shop around until they find a job that allows them to do just that. When the economy rebounds, Gen Y will have a choice about where to work because there aren't quite enough of them to fill the jobs that will be available.

If you're a Boomer reading this, you're no doubt thinking, "Life's not fair." You're right. Members of Gen Y simply don't have to do what you did to get ahead. Step back and learn something from them. Gen Y is bringing something to the workplace that no other generation has before. This generation has the ability to turn business on its head. To that end, as mentioned earlier, they interview potential employers more than these employers interview them!

Corporate America will either embrace this changing dynamic or it won't succeed, and embracing this dynamic means embracing inclusion, which is critical to retaining Gen Y employees.

THE LATTICE VS. THE LADDER

In their book *The Corporate Lattice*, Cathleen Benko and Molly Anderson build a case for the death of the traditional corporate ladder and the emergence of a new organizational structure—the corporate lattice—that is flatter and more collaborative and that serves to meet the needs of the changing workforce.

The corporate lattice, say Benko and Anderson, impacts the way work gets done, the way participation is fostered, and the way careers are built. Importantly, lattice organizations nurture transparent cultures, providing many opportunities for employees in all parts of the organization to provide input, feedback, and ideas.

Benko and Anderson point out the benefits of the flattening of organizations, but this flattening also poses a new challenge: it makes lateral career opportunities much harder to come by. In order to keep your employees engaged and hopeful about their future at your organization, you must continue to offer lateral opportunities. This will not only keep them excited about their jobs but will also give them more experience with different parts of the organization so, that when additional opportunities come along, they'll be ready.

Today's employees, particularly Generation Y, know how valuable they are. They know they have great ideas and viewpoints to share, and they want to be heard. Keeping the decision-making process in the hands of a few top executives shut away in their ivory towers will not fly with employees anymore. An old dentists' adage says, "Ignore your teeth, and they'll go away." The same can be said about employees in today's workforce. Employees who feel like their opinions aren't included in the discussion will simply transition to more inclusive work environments, possibly with one of your competitors.

While you might be telling yourself that the current job market will help you keep your employees, the economy won't be down forever. According to the Deloitte LLP 2010 Ethics & Workplace Survey,[2] thirty-four percent of employed Americans plan to look for a new job once the economy turns around.

If your company already has a strong culture of inclusion, you might not need to worry too much about that figure. If you aren't a particularly inclusive company, you should be very afraid. Your employees might already be plotting their escape from what they see as a dead-end environment in which they don't feel appreciated.

As mentioned previously, losing and replacing employees creates real costs. According to the Korn/Ferry Institute in *The War for Talent: Myths and Realities*, the economics of losing good talent is high. Specifically, the cost of replacing an employee is 100 to 150 percent of a person's salary including the recruiting costs, loss of productivity, benefits, opportunity, and relocation costs. And Korn/Ferry points out this doesn't include "the intelligence deficit that occurs when knowledge about company processes and technologies walks out the door."[3]

Here's how to avoid this scenario:

1. **Build the bridge between generations.** Make room for Gen Y. Knowledge workers are techno savvy and they want to have more of a say and to move up faster. Have them work with Baby Boomers or Traditionalists in a reverse mentoring way that has twofold benefits: Boomers or Traditionalists can teach Gen Y about the organization while Gen Y can help Boomers/Traditionalists keep up on their technology skills.

2. **Determine who your "keepers" are.** Who are the best and brightest? Challenge yourself to go beyond those who have traditionally been in key positions in the past.

3. **Let command and control management die a fast death.** Remember that everyone has something to bring to the table. Stop telling people what to do and instead ask for their input for better business results. This feeling of ownership in the company's success will help you keep your best talent.

4. **Remember that today's talent in all generations is highly skilled and adept at solving complex business problems.** These individuals don't need to be told

how to solve problems. Let them work individually or collaboratively.

5. **Make talent planning a key priority for your business.** Examine not only who is working in your environment but also who should be. Who do you need to grow your business into new and emerging markets? Who do you need to create a collaborative and inclusive work environment? Include underrepresented and underutilized groups.

6. **Social media is your friend.** Start seeing Facebook, Twitter, and other social media as business resources rather than security threats and time wasters. Today's workforce learns not from being handed content but rather from utilizing connections.

7. **Get diversity of thought.** Make sure the right people are in the room, particularly those affected by the decision or closest to the work. This means going beyond the traditional group of people who are there. Really think about who could bring valuable input to the process.

8. **Look for "lattice" opportunities for leadership development.** With the flattening of organizations, the traditional steps of learning have gone away. Build skills through cross-functional assignments.

Inclusion is the solution to retention in today's ever-changing workplace. Every time an employee walks out your door and, potentially, into the door of a competitor, you lose. You lose human capital, you lose institutional knowledge, and you lose brainpower. If you're not thinking every day about how you can retain the staff you have—and *doing something to make it happen*—you lose. And, as we've seen, there is a lot to lose in the volatile business environment of the twenty-first century.

Endnotes

1. http://www.forbes.com/sites/danschawbel/2011/11/22/whos-at-fault-for-high-gen-y-turnover/.

2. http://www.deloitte.com/us/ethicssurvey.

3. *The War for Talent: Myths and Reality.* The Korn/Ferry International Institute, 2008.

9
Inclusion Is the Solution to Innovation

Today organizations are realizing that diversity includes all the ways we are unique, but inclusion is how we leverage those unique characteristics to drive innovation and growth for both our businesses and our employees.

Clydie Douglass,
Director Diversity and Inclusion,
3M

There was a period of time where you could get away with a little less than optimum performance and still succeed. In the current environment, you've got very little margin for error, creating greater urgency around ensuring you leverage every employee.

Kim Koonce,
HR Executive,
formerly of Pepsico and Energy Future Holdings

INCLUSION

The best innovator in the world today seems to be Apple. Apple revolutionized computing (Macintosh), digital media (Pixar), tablets (iPad), how we listen to music (iPod and iTunes), and turned our phones into total mobile devices (iPhone), to name just a few accomplishments. At every step of the way, Steve Jobs knew the competitors would soon be at his heels. Think about the tablet explosion that has occurred as a result of the iPad's popularity. Think about the explosion of Android phones that came after the iPhone launched.

Even Apple, in today's fast-changing, increasingly global environment, needs to constantly innovate. You can't rest on your laurels and hope to thrive off one great innovation. You can't afford to sit back and keep doing what has always worked in the past, because your competitors will copy you; they will improve on what has worked for you and they will come up with new ways to do business that will make your current practices obsolete.

How do organizations keep up with the ongoing cycle of competition? Where does this much innovation come from? As the Center for American Progress has pointed out, "Most people believe that innovation requires smarter people, better ideas. That premise, though intuitive, omits what may be the most powerful but least understood force for innovation: diversity."[1]

Diversity of people and diversity of thought can remain untapped without a culture of inclusion. Creating that culture is critical for those who wish to harvest innovative ideas.

While numerous arguments can be made in support of inclusion as a driver of innovation, they all boil down to two factors. First, inclusion brings in a variety of inputs that help identify ongoing unmet needs that require innovative solutions. Second, inclusion brings in a variety of viewpoints shaped by diverse past experiences, cultural backgrounds, individual knowledge, and unique thought processes that lay the broadest base for potential ideas.

To better understand the importance of the first factor, consider where organizations look when trying to understand market needs and identify areas where innovation can tap into unmet demand. According to the 2011 BoozCo Global Innovation 1000 study, innovative companies employ three core strategies:

- "Need seekers" engage current and potential customers and seek to identify unarticulated needs and create new products and services.
- "Market readers" watch both customers and competitors and take a more incremental approach to innovation by tweaking existing products and services to better fit the needs of the market.
- "Technology drivers" try to leverage their existing technology to create breakthrough solutions to address unmet customer needs.[2]

While each of these strategies takes a somewhat different approach to developing innovative products and services, they all start at the same place: trying to understand customer needs. Most of the companies involved in the Global Innovation 1000 study recognized the importance of connecting with all potential customers. In fact, over sixty percent saw "strong identification with the customer" as an important cultural attribute for innovation, more than any other attribute.[3] That's hardly surprising, but what wasn't addressed in the study was how, if at all, these companies used inclusion and diversity as strategies to identify with and anticipate the needs of their customers.

It seems like a no-brainer. As America becomes more diverse, customers become more diverse. Similarly, an increasingly global marketplace greatly expands the realm of possible customers and the realm of differences among those customers.

Identifying with customers, then, means you identify not only with blue-collar Caucasian families in Indiana but first- or second-generation Hispanic families in Texas as well as young, tech-savvy Chinese college students in Beijing.

Wouldn't it be much easier to identify with these diverse groups if you had members of those groups working for you? Why ask your North American employees to guess what new products or services the South Americans are interested in when you can just go down the hall and talk to your South American employees?

Clarence Nunn, President and CEO of GE Capital Fleet Services, puts it this way: "Eventually, when you're sitting around that board table and not everyone looks the same, all of a sudden the richness of the dialogue is taken to a new level and questions get asked that would not have ordinarily been asked."

Clearly, identifying unmet or unarticulated needs is only half the innovation battle. Indeed, many of the most pressing issues facing organizations are already well known, like how do we reduce costs in the production process? How do we increase product usability? How do we add value to customers without drastically changing our service model?

Companies that can consistently answer these questions and meet the needs and wants of their customers will be in great shape to compete effectively, even in the most dynamic markets. And just as inclusion is the solution to identifying where innovation is needed, inclusion is the solution for driving continuous effective innovation.

INNOVATION ON THE EDGE

As Yann Cramer of Innovation Excellence points out in his article "Diversity Is a Source of Creativity and Resilience," innovation rarely happens at the core of any discipline, whether it's technology, business, music, or any other realm. It usually isn't the "traditionalists" at the heart of their field who find groundbreaking new ways of doing things. Instead, innovation happens at the edges of a discipline, where traditional viewpoints are challenged or complemented with knowledge from other areas of study.[4]

A MULTITUDE OF LENSES

When I am faced with a problem, I have a unique way of attempting to solve it based on my past experiences, my educational background, and the cultural influences that shape how I look at the world. This is the lens through which I see the world, so this is the lens through which I approach problem-solving. You have your own lens, as does every employee in your company. These multiple lenses reflect a great value to your organization (pun intended). The more lenses through which your company can view a problem, the more likely you are to find a unique, innovative solution.

On the other hand, if your employees have nearly identical educational, cultural, and demographic backgrounds, you're likely to find that their perspectives are very similar as well, offering you access to fewer lenses. This is precisely why diversity is so important for innovation. If you have a multitude of lenses through which to view your world, you're going to have a multitude of ideas about how the world should and will look in the future and how to position your organization to be competitive in that future.

EMBRACE YOUR DIVERSITY

While many organizations seek out diverse employees, once these employees are hired, they are often expected to set aside their individuality and focus on a team identity.

This is a mistake.

In 2003, University of Texas psychology professor Bill Swann set up an experiment to evaluate how diverse teams work together. Swann and his team divided four hundred MBA students into teams of four to six individuals with diverse backgrounds. Swann's initial theory was that groups composed of diverse individuals could use their diverse viewpoints and collective knowledge and expertise to create better outcomes than groups lacking diversity. Swann further hypothesized that to be more effective, these individuals should downplay their personal identities and create more of a team identity.

While the first half of the theory proved true, the second half did not. Swann found that, "Expressing personal identities in groups seems to have beneficial effects because those who express themselves are more likely to feel known and understood, because they actually are better known and understood." He adds, "Feeling known and understood causes people to open up, which can foster creative solutions to problems confronting the group."[5]

INCLUSION TRUMPS ABILITY

The Center for American Progress makes a strong argument for the value of inclusion within a diverse group of individuals relative to simply putting a group of smart people together. As discussed earlier, diverse people have diverse lenses through which they see the world and look at problems. When allowed to complement one another, these lenses can create entirely new heuristics, or common methods of addressing problems, whereas a homogeneous group of very smart people will simply be better at using the lens they all started with.

Consider a color analogy. If Person A sees the world through a blue lens and Person B sees the world through a yellow lens, having them collaborate allows you to look at a problem in blue, yellow, or green (i.e., blue + yellow). However, if you have two Person A's, you simply have a deeper blue.

In other words, ten Albert Einsteins probably aren't as good at solving problems and innovating as one Steve Jobs, one Einstein, and one Da Vinci.

COMMUNICATE TO INNOVATE

Having a diverse range of viewpoints and insights is crucial for innovation, and your ability to utilize those diverse viewpoints increases exponentially when you have robust communication. If you have ten diverse individuals working separately on a project, you benefit from ten different viewpoints. When you include all of these people in one discussion, you benefit from a sharing of ideas in which one group member can use her unique perspective to build off an undeveloped thought from another group member. Likewise, a wide array of experiences and knowledge can help the group think critically and avoid "groupthink," the tendency for a group of like-minded people to be so concerned about maintaining harmony that they overlook creative alternatives.

AND THE INNOVATORS? GEN Y

Everyone can innovate. Every gender, every age group, every ethnicity. All can be brilliant. All can be creative. But if I have to tip my hat to the future superstar of innovation in the workforce of tomorrow, it's Generation Y, hands down.

Gen Y represents the new wave of modern employees. This group is poised to replace the Baby Boomers as the dominant demographic age group over the coming decade, and the personality of this group is going to force employers to work extra hard to engage them. But what is so great about Gen Y? Why should organizations feel obligated to spend so much time and effort engaging this group? What's wrong with the traditional approaches to engagement that have worked just fine with the Baby Boomers?

For starters, the business world of the future will belong to Gen Y, and companies looking to succeed in that new world absolutely have to include Gen Y in planning for it. The speed with which the global economy and business world are changing cannot be overstated. Today's competitive landscape is increasingly influenced by decision-makers and markets from around the globe, and as time goes by, this globalization will only continue to spread. Gen Y represents the best weapon available to many organizations as they transition into an increasingly global environment, so it is critical that organizations learn how to get the most from this new generation. And the importance of knowledge workers to an organization has grown steadily in recent years and shows no signs of slowing.

To be blunt, Gen Y is best equipped and best personifies the characteristics that companies will need to be successful in this changing arena. They can lead those companies' transformations to knowledge-based, globally competitive organizations. And what better way to foster innovation than by taking advantage of such a collaborative group of employees? Members of Gen Y have shown that they are not only able to be inclusive and collaborative but are also willing to do so. These young workers appreciate the importance of bringing in diverse viewpoints and do so readily.

Ultimately, inclusion is key to innovation because inclusion increases the collective brain of an organization, adding new ideas and allowing those ideas to interact, combine, and improve. Diverse ideas are key to this process, and business leaders need to remember that innovation doesn't happen in the comfort zone of any discipline. It happens at the fringes, where diverse viewpoints challenge the status quo and provide new solutions to old problems.

But diversity alone is not enough. It's just the starting point. You can hire the most diverse workforce imaginable, but to be truly innovative, you must be collaborative and inclusive. It's not enough to simply *have* diversity among your employees—you must capitalize on that diversity through inclusion. Problem-solving techniques and problem solvers themselves build off one another. Indeed, they *thrive* off one another. Bringing in people with a wide array of experiences, skills, insights, and thought processes creates a rich environment for creativity and innovation, but only if you seek their perspectives and actually listen to them!

The whole is greater than the sum of its parts, and a diverse group of creative thinkers will outperform a homogenous group of similar-minded geniuses. The key is to be diverse, to be inclusive, and to foster effective communication.

Endnotes

1. http://www.americanprogress.org/issues/2007/01/diversity_powers_innovation.html.

2. http://www.booz.com/media/uploads/BoozCo-Global-Innovation-1000-2011-Culture-Key.pdf.

3. http://www.booz.com/media/uploads/BoozCo-Global-Innovation-1000-2011-Culture-Key.pdf.

4 http://www.innovationexcellence.com/blog/2011/01/28/diversity-is-a-source-of-creativity-and-resilience/.

5 http://www.inc.com/guides/2011/01/how-to-foster-innovation-through-diverse-workgroups.html.

10
Inclusion Embraces the Global Mindset

You need to design a diversity and inclusion framework that's general enough to provide consistent guidelines and yet give each market economy freedom that allows them to connect their efforts to drive the localized business growth.

Donald Fan,
Senior Director, Global Office of Diversity,
Walmart

Our focus is on meeting the needs of our customers in every one of our stores. Each store, each market is going to have its own unique make-ups that are relevant to those markets. For us, it's really making sure that we have a team in place at each of those locations that is able to meet the needs of the customers in that market.

Shanequa Williams,
Human Capital Business Partner,
Select Comfort Corporation

It should be no secret to anyone reading this book that we are living in an increasingly global, interconnected, and diverse world. In the early twentieth century, an American producer or service provider could get along just fine focusing on the American market or even a regional or state market. Even if a company wanted to enter a foreign market, the logistical challenges would have dissuaded all but the most ambitious. Similarly, domestic organizations had little to fear from competitors abroad, but those days are long gone.

In "Redrawing the Map: Globalization and the Changing World of Business," Ernst & Young identify two major factors shaping the modern business landscape: the movement of capital from developed to developing markets and global demographic change.[1]

Examples are all around us. Today, Japanese, European, Korean, Indian, and American auto manufacturers all compete to sell cars in South America. A British financial services company might rely on an American advertising agency to market its investment services in the Middle East. Markets within our own borders advertise tastes and preferences that were once considered "foreign." All this means that thinking locally or even nationally will not cut it anymore. In a global market, the only mindset that will suffice is a global mindset.

The Ernst & Young report also surveyed 520 senior business executives and interviewed thirty senior executives/prominent experts to analyze the changing international landscape and explore what companies must do to compete in the new global marketplace. Not surprisingly, inclusion was one of the principal success factors identified.[2]

NEW RULES, NEW GAME

In the 1960s, if you asked one hundred people from around the world where cars were made, you'd likely get the same answer every time: the United States. American auto companies once had a nearly global monopoly on automobile production. Everyone wanted big, fast American cars. That all changed when gas prices began to climb because the answer to rising fuel costs didn't come from Ford, Chevy, or GM. It came from Japan. The already globalizing economy allowed Japanese companies like Toyota to tap into America's market with small, fuel-efficient cars. Japan changed the game. They were able to do so because the rules had changed. Globalization meant that new ideas and new business models could originate from across the Pacific Ocean. Americans no longer had to rely on the Big Three to give them fuel-efficient cars.

The globalization of the auto market is just one example of the ability of foreign companies to rise up and change the game. Companies need to find ways to respond to the threats and opportunities created by newly developing nations, which present both new markets and new competitors. According to Donald Sull, Professor of Management Practice at the London Business School, companies often use one of two strategies to manage the globalization challenge: absorption and agility. Both strategies can benefit enormously from a culture of inclusion.[3]

According to Sull, absorption is the strategy typically best suited to companies in large developed countries such as the United States. These companies have established brands, large production capacity, technology, and the ability to diversify. Using these resources, large companies can respond to threats from abroad by simply absorbing new technologies, new products, and new ways of doing business. In other words, they can sit and wait for new innovations to emerge and then mimic them.

Smaller companies, on the other hand, particularly those in developing nations, have to rely on agility, the ability to change direction quickly in a dynamic business environment. A highly agile company can change its brand or convert its capital from one production method to another with relative ease at a fairly low cost. Agility comes from getting everyone on board with what's going on and where the business is going.

While these two strategies both have their advantages, Sull suggests agility may have the edge. He says, "To me the striking thing is how fast agility can trump absorption." However, this does not mean that large, complex companies in developed nations are stuck with a second best business strategy.

To successfully absorb new developments in the global business environment, it is crucial to have an inclusive culture. The more diverse knowledge sets you can include in your strategic planning, the faster you can identify and respond to new developments. If nobody on your upper management team knows anything about East Asia, you can easily be blindsided by new developments in that region. By the time these developments are significant enough to get your attention, it may be too late.

To be agile, a company needs to have an innovative culture. It needs to be able to come up with creative new ways to make transitions and efficiently convert resources from one use to another. As I discussed in Chapter 9, inclusive cultures utilize their diverse knowledge, backgrounds, and thought processes to create an environment that thinks outside the box and breeds creativity.

Clarence Nunn, President and CEO of GE Capital Fleet Services, reflects that, "I don't think a Hispanic buys from other

Hispanics just because they're Hispanic. If you have a poor product, people aren't going to buy it. I think that the formula of that product, the marketing of that product, the identifying of the target market—that's what's important. So if you are a company that says, 'We are dead-set on going into China,' how important is it to have people that understand the culture, have grown up in the culture, experienced the culture, and know the pitfalls? These people have to be at the table!"

OUT OF THE IVORY TOWER

Years ago, American companies like McDonald's created products catered to American appetites and the rest of the world literally ate them up. Hollywood movies, created for American audiences, based on American culture, were in high demand around the globe. While there is certainly still a demand for American culture and American products, developing countries now want to consume goods and services that reflect their own local tastes. And the increased ability of domestic companies to give them just that means America's monopoly on consumers is a thing of the past. The emergence of Bollywood is a prime example.

India, one of the world's fastest growing economies and largest markets, has developed its own sophisticated entertainment industry. As nations around the world develop the capacity to meet the demands of their populations, foreign companies will have to cater to the unique needs of local groups.

Inclusion is key to satisfying these diverse markets. If you are a culturally homogenous organization struggling to break into the Brazilian market, you shouldn't be surprised. How can you hope to compete with local firms or diverse, inclusive multinational firms if you don't understand the culture or the market you are trying to lure over to your products or services?

Companies that employ a variety of diverse individuals have a great advantage over those that don't, and this doesn't just mean middle management. You need sophisticated executives with a diversity of backgrounds to help you coordinate your global strategy because every aspect of your business has to be able to successfully navigate a range of cultures and tastes. For example, it's not just about figuring out what type of food people like in your target market. What is a hilarious commercial in one country might be extremely offensive in another. What is polite when dealing with one country's regulators might be aloof or rude to regulators in another nation.

WE GET IT . . . SORT OF

Companies today increasingly recognize the importance of increasing the diversity of their top management. As the following chart shows, close to fifty percent of the executives surveyed by Ernst & Young saw the level of international experience of their workforce as an important cultural factor in doing business internationally.

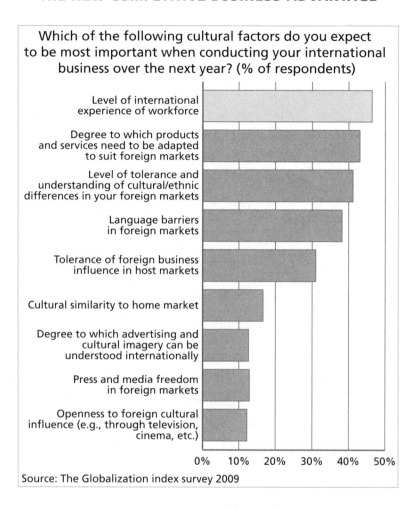

Which of the following cultural factors do you expect to be most important when conducting your international business over the next year? (% of respondents)

Source: The Globalization index survey 2009

At the same time, these executives admitted to a dearth of geographic diversity on their boards of directors. Forty-five percent of the companies surveyed that were operating in at least twenty-five countries had at most a couple of foreign nationals on their boards of directors. In roughly one-third of the companies surveyed, less than five percent of all senior management at the company headquarters was a foreign national.[4]

Clearly, there is a disconnect between recognizing the importance of inclusion in the global marketplace and actually implementing the needed changes. Companies that are global need to become truly global citizens. This means they need to have a global composition, not just in the local offices of the countries they operate in but also in their corporate headquarters.

GLOBAL CITIZENSHIP

"Global citizenship" is a term used by Jeanne Meister and Karie Willyerd that involves "understanding how to conduct business in a foreign country, developing an increased cultural intelligence and a deeper appreciation of the relationship between business and society, and being able to understand complex policy environments and how to work in virtual teams with people from all over the world."[5]

The changes I am seeing today in business that I talked about at the beginning of this book—changes related to technology, automation, globalization, and the economy—all require new conversations. Collectively, we need new and more varied voices at the table. Sameness of individuals and thoughts within organizations does not lead to innovation and business success. Sameness yields mediocrity and lack of imagination. Sameness leaves us disconnected from emerging markets and emerging ways of thinking. It leaves us in the dust. If we're not part of the new conversations and if we're not having these conversations with the broad array of constituencies that represent our markets, we will not survive in the new global business normal.

Endnotes

1. http://www.ey.com/GL/en/Issues/Business-environment/
   Redrawing-the-map--globalization-and-the-changing-world-of-
   business---Five-business-responses-to-globalization.

2. Ibid.

3. http://www.businessresearch.eiu.com/sites/default/files/
   Redrawing%20the%20map%20-%20WEF.pdf.

4. http://www.managementthinking.eiu.com/sites/default/files/
   Redrawing%20the%20map%20-%20WEF.pdf.

5. *The 2020 Workplace.* Jeanne C. Meister and Karie Willyerd. New
   York: Harper Collins, 2010.

11

Insights Shared by Champions of Inclusion

nclusionINC has been championing inclusion as a solution to business success for more than ten years. Along the way, I've been fortunate to work with a growing number of senior executives who also believe that inclusion takes the focus on diversity to the next level. I've shared some of their comments throughout the book. Here I provide more in-depth perspectives from these various champions of inclusion.

INCLUSION IS DIFFERENT THAN DIVERSITY

The inclusion piece, in my mind, is the most important. I call it the engine that drives diversity. I can go out and hire diverse employees all day long, but if I'm not inclusive in my organization—if I don't include those diverse employees—forget it. They're not going to stay. I'm trying to make Halliburton a more inclusive organization first, not a more diverse organization. I feel that if you make it inclusive, diversity will come.

Cindy Bigner,
Director, Global Diversity and Inclusion,
Halliburton

Organizations for many years saw diversity as compliance. Today organizations are realizing that diversity includes all the ways we are unique, but inclusion is how we leverage those unique characteristics to drive innovation and growth for both our businesses and our employees. If you only focus on the numbers, leaders can feel beaten up or discouraged with the lack of progress. I believe if you focus on changing the work environment by developing leaders and implementing systems and processes to create a more inclusive work environment that also focuses on the development of talent, you will begin to see change that is sustainable.

Clydie Douglass,
Director Diversity and Inclusion,
3M

We promote diversity of thought—that means our view of diversity is a little bit different. It's far beyond just the race, the gender, and ethnicity. It's really about different kinds of perspectives, ideas, styles, experiences, strengths, and values and how you really leverage those differences so you can reap the value of diversity. We try to better understand diversity beyond the traditional definition—we invite differences and invite our associates to bring the whole self to the workplace. For us, diversity is really about counting people and inclusion is really about making people count.

Donald Fan,
Senior Director, Global Office of Diversity,
Walmart

It's really not about traditional diversity or the Equal Employment Opportunity Commission. It has to do with business. It has to do with people learning to be open and to accept a variety of people and their thoughts and ideas. The example I give is that I worked in a company where there were a lot of long-tenured people. The exclusion there was not based on race and gender but on tenure within the organization. It was discrimination; it just wasn't illegal! Think of the people at organizations who are minimized because of their age—whether they're older or younger than the average group.

Inclusion is now the sort of capitalized work—it's really now about how we go about including everybody. Now that you have diversity, how are you going to make it as productive as possible through inclusion?

Kim Koonce,
HR Executive,
formerly of Pepsico and Energy Future Holdings

I think diversity has gotten really pigeonholed around ethnicity and it's not as much a conversation around bringing your whole self as it needs to be. I think there's a fine nuance between inclusion and diversity. Some would look at inclusion as probably broader. Whether you're a white male or not, you can be included in any particular inclusion initiative. Whereas diversity, just because of the legacy of it, everybody thinks that it's really around somebody's skin color or ethnicity.

Clarence Nunn,
President and CEO,
GE Capital Fleet Services

One of the things I'm a big proponent of is that diversity and inclusion are great, but they don't go far enough. I talk about diversity, inclusion, and equality. Diversity means you get invited to the party. Inclusion means you get a seat at the table. Equality means you get the same thing on your plate in terms of opportunity as everybody else. Too often if you leave it at just the diversity conversation or the inclusion conversation and the equality impact is left out, you can still have holes in your strategies.

Keith Wyche,
President and CEO,
Cub Foods

INCLUSION STARTS AT THE TOP

[At GE] it started with Jack Welch and has continued on through our current chairman Jeff Immelt. Jeff has an Affinity Council—a global diversity council—that consists of him and many of his peer leaders. On a quarterly basis we meet with all the affinity groups (AGs) and Jeff and have a candid dialogue about what we are doing around things like recruitment, retention, development, and all of those aspects of how you become a better company around diversity. Does the chairman have a voice in the process? Does he have his key leaders involved in the process? Then how far down in the organization are those key initiatives known?

Clarence Nunn,
President and CEO,
GE Capital Fleet Services

You need to have a top to bottom understanding of diversity. Organizations I have worked with that are really sincere about it do a few things. They make it a part of their culture. What I mean by that is they support business resource groups, they actually have metrics for key executives based on diversity deliverables, they have mandates for job titles at the director level, and above all they have a diverse slate of candidates or interview a diverse slate of candidates before making a hire and they have development programs in place. Those are the things that companies further along the continuum do that a lot of companies don't.

Keith Wyche,
President and CEO,
Cub Foods

INCLUSION IS ABOUT BUSINESS

There is philanthropy that companies take on but, certainly for publicly traded companies, we're here to support our stockholders. We need to challenge diversity and inclusion to not be just the right thing to do but make it the right business thing to do. It's all focused on generating a return on investment for the individual, for the company. If that becomes our framework, I think that this conversation has a lot of staying power.

I've seen it move from being a slogan to actually being the way some companies really work. Many companies have Affinity Groups; many will sponsor events. They'll ask senior leaders to attend these events and then, once that happens, 'check the box' and go back to business as usual. Diversity and inclusion have to work both ways— they have to be part of your business strategy and you have to treat it like any other business process. That's the only way it becomes a part of the way you work.

Clarence Nunn,
President and CEO,
GE Capital Fleet Services

For a time there it was hard to quantify the business case. But as the world has gone more global and as organizations are looking to get new customers and clientele, the business case has become very apparent. You don't want to leave money on the table or lose money. If I'm going to grow, I have to understand my customers.

Keith Wyche,
President and CEO,
Cub Foods

INCLUSION LEADS TO EMPLOYEE ENGAGEMENT

Many studies have been done that show that a team of people who are very similar are not as creative or as effective as a team that has a mix of experiences, background, and education. If you encourage the input of the person who has a different perspective or doesn't follow the 'groupthink,' you will have a stronger outcome.

Clydie Douglass,
Director Diversity and Inclusion,
3M

Internally we have what we call the associate portal—we publish a blog. We want to hear the different conversations, what's on their minds. Our CEO has a monthly town hall meeting open to all home office associates. He shares business initiatives, and at the end, employees can ask questions. It gives us kind of a gauge to tell what the engagement levels are. All of those different channels then allow us to hear the voices so we can make sure we listen and also, more importantly, that we hear. Then we can respond or react to issues.

Donald Fan,
Senior Director, Global Office of Diversity,
Walmart

If you have a women's group or an African American group or an Asian group, what you're doing is creating groups for people who are different but not including other folks in the dialogue. That's where the train kind of stops. Because you've got white men who, frankly, every place I go they're the ones at the top of the organizational chart. But they're not included in these dialogues. By not including them, we are actually behaving in a way that excludes people. We're almost minimizing them or not including them in our conversations.

Kim Koonce,
HR Executive,
formerly of Pepsico and Energy Future Holdings

As cliché as it may sound, you really don't know where a good idea may come from. You really don't. So, I do this thing where I'll sit down, whether in customer service or the maintenance department, with employees to see what their day is like. How does their job work? I think that as companies, it's important for people to feel like they have a voice because that's the only way they rally around a strategy. You have to create an environment where people feel they can't hide and where they believe they have a voice in the process.

Clarence Nunn,
President and CEO,
GE Capital Fleet Services

Companies have done a great job of recruiting and attracting diverse talent, but they don't always incorporate it operationally within the organization or have the infrastructure to support it. Here's an analogy I use: I love fish, and the most beautiful fish in the world are saltwater fish. You can pay $1000.00 or more for one of these fish, but if you put that saltwater fish in fresh water, it won't survive. Some companies' diversity and inclusion efforts are like that. You can get the best and the brightest, but you can't put them in an environment where they can't thrive. That whole area of retention and development is something that companies struggle with.

Keith Wyche,
President and CEO,
Cub Foods

INCLUSION LEADS TO CUSTOMER CONNECTIONS

As a company, we put forth a lot of effort to make sure we are nationalized as much as possible. That means we hire local nationals from countries wherever possible. That creates a whole different view, if you will, or a whole different challenge as it relates to inclusion because, as you well know, people tend to want to hire people who look like them and act like them.

Cindy Bigner,
Director, Global Diversity and Inclusion,
Halliburton

The global economy and emerging markets create unique opportunities and challenges for global companies. The idea of diversity and inclusion is both global and local. I believe the changes are forward moving but continue to be more complex as we consider the layers of diversity beyond race, gender, sexual orientation, physical ability, etc. and consider the cultural, social, and economic contexts of each person's life journey.

Clydie Douglass,
Director Diversity and Inclusion,
3M

We look at how we can truly enhance these competencies around a global culture—how we can be sensitive and able to lead with the nuances from the culture perspective as well as be open-minded and nimble. We want to replicate the success from the U.S. model and yet make sure our efforts or initiatives truly address the localized business challenge. Companies need to be able to adjust their business strategies when operating in a different culture in a different country or different markets.

Donald Fan,
Senior Director, Global Office of Diversity,
Walmart

My philosophy for running my stores is that, even though the name is Cub Foods, I'm a neighborhood grocer. So each neighborhood is different. One of the things I do in this role is give each of my store directors a demographic breakdown of who is in a two-mile radius— their income and ethnic breakdown. This is the first step in helping understand everything from hiring decisions to marketing, because if you're a heavily Hmong community, you want to have someone there who can relate to Hmong people, who can tell you what they like and don't like—that's how it makes a difference in my space.

Keith Wyche,
President and CEO,
Cub Foods

Today, our efforts need to be replicated or expanded into the different markets we have operations around. Each market has its own culture, history, traditions, and ways of doing business—also a different base of customers. You need to design a diversity and inclusion framework that's general enough to provide consistent guidelines and yet give each market economy freedom that allows them to connect their efforts to drive the localized business growth.

Donald Fan,
Senior Director, Global Office of Diversity,
Walmart

INCLUSION IMPACTS CAN— AND SHOULD—BE MEASURED

I definitely think that you can show ROI. I think that we can show changes in turnover, year to year; we measure litigation on EEOC charges within the U.S., and also internationally. Making better hiring decisions really has an impact on ROI—hiring the right people so that you're maximizing the training time.

We can look at it from a training perspective. It's a bit more difficult, but we put value on the amount of training that our employees receive, and personally, I think that we can show that if we add to those training hours diversity and inclusion training, we can show that we're exerting this amount of money on efforts as it relates to turnover and the engagement we're seeing.

Cindy Bigner,
Director, Global Diversity and Inclusion,
Halliburton

We are now at a place where we can't not face these sensitivities and have real conversations about why this is in place, what it is going to benefit, and then have hard metrics. Not 'How many I've hired,' but 'What is the value proposition? What is the return on investment?'

Clarence Nunn,
President and CEO,
GE Capital Fleet Services

You measure the success of diversity and inclusion in two ways. One will be the best business solution because it engages all kinds of perspectives, all kinds of ideas and thoughts. On the other side will be highly engaged associates within a more productive team environment. If you have those two pieces, that means you have success with your diversity and inclusion efforts that will call you out compared to your competitors.

Donald Fan,
Senior Director, Global Office of Diversity,
Walmart

When I look at the careers of any individuals, there are three components that matter and make up how successful they'll be. First and foremost is performance—that's table stakes. The second piece, and this is where diversity and inclusion can play a big role, is what I call exposure. Are these people exposed to the right information, the right leaders, and the right processes? Then it's perception, because what happens is many times your reputation goes before you get into the room. So diversity and inclusion, if done properly, really enhance all three.

Keith Wyche,
President and CEO,
Cub Foods

12

Inclusion As a
Business Strategy

It is not about any color except green!

Clarence Nunn, President and CEO,
GE Capital Fleet Services

When I asked a group of senior-level managers point-blank, what is it going to take to make you understand how important inclusion is, everyone said 'show me the value-show me the bottom line-show me how it impacts revenue.'

Cindy Bigner, Director, Global Diversity and Inclusion,
Halliburton

Many organizations talk about embracing change, but the actual business of change moves forward when your leaders walk, talk, live and breathe it. If it's driven from the top down, change will happen.

Kim Koonce, HR Executive,
formerly of Pepsico and Energy Future Holdings

By now, I hope I have built a case for inclusion as a linchpin to your business success. In today's world, there is no such thing as "business as usual." Your markets, your employees, your customers, and your competitors are all constantly changing. If you fail to connect to the ongoing current of change, you *will* be swept away.

If you want to succeed in this brave new world of business, you will have to not only cope with these changes but also embrace them and turn them to your advantage. I suggest that the way to embrace change is to embrace inclusion as a business strategy. While there is much you can't control, there is one very important thing you *can* control: actively including the voices, the ideas, and the passions of your employees and your customers. You can choose inclusion.

Yet sadly, many organizations are still focused on affirmative action-like metrics. They're still putting groups of people into categories, counting how many they have in each group, and calling these numbers their "inclusion and diversity metrics." I.e., when I've asked senior executives in Fortune 1000 organizations across the country what their inclusion metrics are, the typical response is, "We count women and people of color."

These numbers may reflect diversity, but I'm here to tell you that these numbers are *not* measures of inclusion . . . or, more importantly, business impact.

Inclusion is not about counting different categories of employees, yet that is what most organizations tend to do as they focus on inclusion and diversity initiatives. Measures of inclusion go beyond counting people to leveraging business results.

When organizations wish to increase revenue, they develop growth strategies to help them accomplish that goal. When they hope to reduce costs, they develop meaningful, measurable objectives along with strategies and tactics to help drive down those costs. Yet when organizations address issues related to inclusion and diversity, their scorecards tend to focus on representation metrics: how many women do we have in leadership positions? How many employees do we have representing certain minority groups?

I'm not saying these organizations should stop counting. Diversity metrics have been and will remain extremely important as part of an overall strategy that links to the bottom line. Yet simply tracking the numbers is a halfhearted effort that only focuses on the population and fails to integrate strengths. It does nothing to address the environment in which people work every day. It does nothing to address what needs to be done to ensure that talent brought into the organization has the expertise and resources to meet business goals.

If inclusion and diversity strategies can't be linked to profitability and productivity, companies won't embrace them for long. Inclusion isn't about simply doing things. It's about *doing things that matter*. And to know what matters, organizations must have metrics that are tied to business imperatives so they can tell whether or not their inclusion behaviors have made a difference.

Cindy Bigner, Director, Global Diversity and Inclusion at Halliburton, comments, "When I asked a group of senior-level managers point-blank, what is it going to take to make you understand how important inclusion is, everyone said 'show me the value-show me the bottom line-show me how it impacts revenue.'"

Talking about the number of certain *types* of people you have hired or who hold certain positions doesn't demonstrate the kind of bottom line value senior leaders are looking for. They're looking for metrics related to how you have decreased turnover, levels of employee engagement gathered through survey data, and specific, bottom-line contributions that employees have made to the organization in terms of increased productivity, new product or service innovations, and growth in existing or new markets.

REALITIES OF THE NEW BUSINESS NORMAL

It is no longer possible to think of your business in local, regional, or even national terms. Even if you don't plan on selling any goods or services beyond your geographic region, you will still be in competition with those who do. Ignore this fact at your peril and remember that:

- **Your customer base is rapidly changing.** Changing demographics means changing tastes and preferences. If you shut yourself off from the groups that will be making up the new American and global consumer landscape, you will fall behind your competitors.
- **Baby Boomers will eventually leave.** As Baby Boomers begin to reach retirement age, their exodus will eventually leave behind a huge gap in the workforce. To replace the aging Boomers, companies will have to turn to the largest cohort to come around since the emergence of the Boomers in the middle of the twentieth century: Gen Y. Unlike previous generations, the value of Generation Y is in their heads, not their arms. If you can't figure out how to be inclusive with this extremely valuable human resource, you will operate at well below peak efficiency.
- **Continuous inward and outward facing innovation is not an option; it's a business imperative.** Competitors are constantly finding new and better ways to reduce

costs, reach newly identified customer cohorts, and improve products. It's not enough to stumble onto one game-changing innovation. Your competitors will soon copy you or come up with the next best thing and render your products or services obsolete. While some businesses might look at these changes and bemoan their situation, others recognize that these changes represent both threats *and* opportunities. Companies that can effectively anticipate and appropriately react to these changes will consistently outperform their competitors.

ONCE AGAIN, INCLUSION IS THE SOLUTION

So how do companies respond to the rapid change around them to ensure their long-term survival? Consider the companies that make up the annual Fortune 500 list. As Jeanne Meister and Karie Willyerd point out, if a company was on the list in 1980, there was a fifty-six percent chance it was still listed in 1994. Leap forward to 2007. In 2007, there was only a thirty percent chance that a company listed in 1994 was still on the list.[1]

Nonetheless, just because *some* companies fail does not mean *all* companies fail. How can you respond to a constantly changing environment and the perpetually increasing impact of the major changes that impact companies today?

Inclusion is the solution. Inclusion within your workforce that strategically involves people of all types and at all levels across the organization. Inclusion within your customer base that strategically understands the needs of people of all types across a global market.

Throughout this book, I have made the case for inclusion as a solution to the increasingly complex challenges facing businesses in this ever-changing world. Whether you are struggling to cope with globalization, worried about how the changing demographics at home will impact your customer base, struggling to find and keep qualified people to counteract the shrinking presence of aging Baby Boomers, or simply trying to keep up with the fast pace of innovation, inclusion is the solution.

Earlier in this chapter, I touched on the impact the fast pace of globalization can have on business. It can be overwhelming to think about doing business in fifty different countries without understanding how to work with their governments, how to create what their people want, and how to effectively market to them. Even in the U.S., as the ethnic make-up of the country remains remarkably dynamic, keeping up with changing trends and catering to diverse groups can be a puzzle. But by seeking out and including talented people with diverse backgrounds, you can better position yourself to manage these changes. For example, it's much easier to understand the market in China if you have Chinese employees in your business.

But how do you find and keep talented, diverse employees when you are struggling to find *anyone* to fill some of your positions? Again, I suggest that inclusion is the solution. Those in Gen Y, the dominant group entering the workforce, have high expectations of the companies they work for. They know they are valuable. They know they have a lot to offer. And they expect to be given a chance to share what they know. In an era of knowledge workers in which a company's most valuable resource lies in the minds of its employees, you absolutely have to let them share. Include them, and you will attract and retain them.

Finally, in today's fast-changing business world, inclusion brings in a variety of viewpoints and mindsets and facilitates a culture willing to challenge the status quo, think outside the box, and be truly innovative. Your employees are your *most valuable asset!* As mentioned earlier, they are human capital, not cattle, so say goodbye to command and control . . .

In his 1960 book *The Human Side of Enterprise*, American social psychologist Douglas McGregor came up with his now widely utilized X-Y theory of management. Theory X holds that the average person is averse to work and therefore must be coerced with threats of punishment to perform assigned tasks. Theory X further holds that most individuals prefer to be directed and have little ambition beyond job security. Clearly, this is a very bleak picture of the workplace.

Theory Y, on the other hand, holds that individuals are motivated by a sense of achievement when succeeding in their jobs and therefore need minimal external control. Theory Y also argues that the capacity for creative thinking and ingenuity exists in the vast majority of employees and that this capacity is largely under-utilized by employers and organizations.[2]

Theories X and Y are two diametrically opposed management styles. While many business leaders would have us believe that Theory X has been replaced by Theory Y, that's delusional thinking. In truth, command and control rather than collaborative management is still part of the culture at many organizations with a marked divide between those who are called on to lend their insights and expertise and those who are simply expected to "do as they're told." Who actually runs these companies? Sometimes it's the traditionalist processes and policies still at play as if the Traditionalists themselves are ghosts in the halls.

As we attempt to respond to a changing world economy and increasingly global marketplace, it is more apparent than ever that we need the commitment and engagement of every member of our workforce if we are to address these emerging challenges. Not surprisingly, successful companies are increasingly experiencing the ability of inclusion to strengthen their businesses.

A 2011 study by i4cp, the Institute for Corporate Productivity, indicated that high performance organizations are three times more likely to devote resources to analyze how an inclusive culture leads to business productivity. According to the study, roughly two-thirds of companies consider inclusion to be part of their overall human resources strategy, yet few of those companies put significant effort into finding an analytical link between inclusion and overall business performance. In other words, inclusion is simply another soft factor for many of these organizations. They say they value inclusion, but they can't articulate or measure its real benefits.[3]

High performing organizations are different. They have moved beyond a command and control style of leadership to an inclusive leadership model that recognizes and values the input of all employees. But as the i4cp research indicates, these companies are still in the minority, and the majority of companies are therefore missing out.

Evan Rosen in "Every Worker Is a Knowledge Worker"[4] recommends five steps that organizations can take to move beyond a command and control structure to benefit from the input of *all*:

- Institute information democracy by giving everyone access to the same data and information
- Break down barriers among levels by giving everybody access to everybody else in the organization

- Use information technology to enable spontaneous collaboration through the adoption of unified communications
- Involve front-line people in decisions—pay everyone to think!
- Recognize and reward broad input; tie raises and promotions to gaining broad input

Why aren't we seeing sweeping changes at organizations around the country as they actively seek to meld the concepts of knowledge and manual workers? Because, despite the oft-stated belief that "Employees are our most valuable asset," most companies are still tied to the old command and control traditions that may have served them in decades past but are woefully inadequate to serve them in the world they exist in today. Profoundly, as Marshall Goldsmith proclaimed in his popular book by the same title, "What got you here won't get you there."

CONCLUSION

While inclusion is important for organizations for a multitude of reasons, at the end of the day, what every organization really cares about is the bottom line. The moral of the story is clear: inclusion is a solution for employee engagement, retention, innovation, productivity and embracing the global mindset. But most of all inclusion is an achievable and urgent business strategy!

Endnotes

1. *The 2020 Workplace.* Jeanne C. Meister and Karie Willyerd. New York: Harper Collins, 2010.

2. http://www.vectorstudy.com/management_theories/theory_X_and_Y.htm.

3. http://www.i4cp.com/news/2011/03/23/i4cp-study-shows-more-top-companies-are-examining-the-business-case-for-inclusion.

4. *BusinessWeek.com.* Accessed January 12, 2011.

About the Author

Shirley Engelmeier has been an Inclusion and Diversity Strategist and Consultant for more than nineteen years. Prior to that, Shirley held senior management positions in global consumer product organizations Brown & Williamson and Frito-Lay. She has pioneered Inclusion and Diversity initiatives that currently have a major impact on improving business results through employee engagement, innovation, productivity and retention. During the past two decades, she introduced significant corporate learning tools such as customized web-based assessments, strategic and customized metrics *beyond* representation and solutions for Learning Over Time®.

INCLUSION

A highly regarded business strategist, Shirley has consulted with Fortune 1000 companies as well as emerging enterprises on Inclusion and Diversity initiatives across a broad range of industries, including SUPERVALU, ESPN, Denny's/Advantica, 3M, R.R. Donnelley, TRW, Prudential, U.S. Bank, COX Communication, BP Pipelines and others. Originally trained as an educator, Shirley earned her B.S. degree from the University of Minnesota and resides with her family in Minneapolis.